You Are
Worthy

A Journey from Despair to Hope

Linda Thompson

ISBN 978-1-64515-988-9 (paperback)
ISBN 978-1-64515-989-6 (digital)

Christian Faith Publishing, Inc.
832 Park Avenue
Meadville, PA 16335
www.christianfaithpublishing.com

Printed in the United States of America

Contents

Acknowledgments

My deepest appreciation to Stephanie Stubblefield, a treasured friend, who cared enough to reach across a table and invite me to a ten week discipleship study. You loved me when I could not love myself and reminded me that My Abba Father is a good, good father. The time spent with you spiraled me forward into recovery.

My heartfelt thanks to Ann Blacktop, my counselor, friend, and guide. You never judged, condemned, or tried to fix me. Instead you listened well, loved me unconditionally, and guided me as I journeyed my way through recovery. You are truly a model of what it means to live life God's way.

And finally, my thanks to Tim Duthler, another counselor and friend. You helped me see life from the perspective of a male, you reminded me often that I am God's daughter, and that He loves me just a I am. Our appointments at the lake in Whitehall have not always been easy, but they have always been a source of wisdom and guidance.

Reflections from Childhood

April 3, 1956, wasn't a typical spring day in western Michigan. The air would normally be crisp and cool, but today, the temperature was just a little warmer and the air more humid than one would expect in early April. Only the radio alerted the community to the drastic change in weather heading straight toward Michigan. As southwest winds began to push hot, humid air into Michigan, the color of the sky changed from a charcoal gray to an eerie greenish-yellow. The wind, once tossing and turning, ceased. Those familiar with dangerous storms no longer needed a radio to alert them. The color of the sky and the stillness of the air were all that was needed to know a storm was very close, a storm that had the potential to destroy everything in its path.

As the winds reached land, tornados began to form. My mother sat on a rocking chair, quietly reading a Bible story, while Dad stood in the bathroom shaving. The radio kept my parents aware of the tornado alert, but when Mom heard the siren, she knew the weather status had been upgraded to a warning.

Dad yelled from the bathroom, "There's a funnel cloud headed in our direction. Get the children downstairs."

My mother whisked my brother, my sister, and I down the stairs and under the table in the southwest corner of the basement. We huddled there while my mother yelled up the stairs.

"Get down here, Frank. I can see the funnel cloud from the window. It's heading straight toward the house!"

"I'll be right down. I am watching it."

"Frank, get down here. Now!"

We couldn't see it from under the table, but the sound was deafening. It could have been a train coming toward the house, but there was no mistaking the distinctive sound of a tornado. My mother called out once again, this time in an angry voice. "Frank!" In what seemed like an instant, my dad was in the basement, and in that same instant, the funnel cloud turned and touched down some miles away. We stayed in the basement as the F-5 tornado blazed a path through Lower Michigan, taking the lives of seventeen people and injuring more than 285.

I remember the musty smell of the blankets that covered the table and the thunderous noise of the tornado. But more than the sights and sounds of the tornado, I remember my mother yelling at my dad. Perhaps it was the first time I had heard her yell at him. Or quite possibly at the age of six, I already knew the consequences of speaking to my dad when he wanted it quiet. His words rang in my ears: "Children are to be seen and not heard."

The sting of my father's hand across my face gave me a clear understanding that I should have no voice. It wasn't what I said; it was that I spoke. That little girl who learned to have no voice still creeps into my life today.

My older brother Dennis remembers as well. He feels the shame of the beatings my father inflicted on both of us. He remembers, as do I, trying to hide but to no avail. When my father was angry, he lashed out at us. Will the little girl inside ever forget the humiliation of my pants being stripped from me and the unmerciful lashing that took place in the moments following?

Memories of my childhood are scarce. I recall my brother forcing me to touch the electric fence and the shock I received when I touched it. I recall the unmerciful tickling, even when I screamed and cried, trying to get him to stop.

I will never forget the pungent smells of the outhouse or the baths we took in the large aluminum washtub. "Mom, can I have my bath first this week?"

"It's your turn next week." It always seemed like it was my turn the next week. The first one in had the clean water, and oh how I longed to have clean water.

It was on the farm, before the deadly tornado, that I learned to be as invisible as possible. The country fields were so inviting. If Dennis went with me, we could run out into them.

We hid in the corn and dodged each other in the hay. One day, we went too far and in the twinkling of an eye, we were lost. My mom recalls the rain-filled ditches and the thought of her children being swallowed up in one of them. She told us more than once, "If you ever get lost, stick together and stay in the same spot. We will look for you. Don't come looking for us."

I heeded her warning even when Dennis wanted to leave me and go looking. "No. Mom said to stay together."

Dennis was determined to do it his way. "They will never find us. You stay here, and I will look."

"Mom told us to stay in one spot. I'm too little. You can't leave me alone."

He finally agreed to stay with me, and within the hour, friends of my father saw us through an opening in the hay. We were scooped up in their arms and carried back to the house. The fear of being lost forever was pale in comparison to the dread of my father's beating. "Spare the rod and spoil the child," he said as his belt came off.

I learned to hide under my bed or in the closet when I saw Dad coming in from the farm. Terror filled my body as I heard his footsteps. Was he here for lunch or had I been bad again?

Did I really think he couldn't find me? When he wanted to, he always did.

My father supported our family by farming but soon discovered that he was very talented in the area of planning and building homes. Before Dennis started going to school, we had moved away from the farm and closer to town into a new home my father had built for our family. No more fields to run in, no more outhouses, and the bathtub was sparkling and white. We still shared bathwater, but the clean tub seemed to make sharing much more tolerable.

I turned six the year the F-5 tornado devastated Michigan. That fall, I entered first grade and met Martha. We were best friends from the first time we met. She wore a hearing aid and didn't speak clearly; thus, the other girls didn't want to play with her. My already broken spirit gravitated immediately to someone else who might be hurting.

The day we were playing, and Martha fell off the swing, ended up hurting me as much as it hurt her. Our teacher Mrs. Scott accused me of pushing her too hard.

I began to cry as I responded. "I didn't push her too hard. I wouldn't hurt her."

"Yes, you did. The other children saw you pushing her."

"But I wasn't pushing her high. Just high enough to make her laugh!"

Martha was quick to defend me. "I was having fun. Lindsey didn't hurt me. My hands slipped, and I fell."

"The girls saw you fall, but they said Lindsey pushed you too hard."

"Please, she didn't make me fall."

I stood silently as Martha pleaded my case. The other girls continued to blame me, and finally, Mrs. Scott took me inside. "You hurt Martha, and you are going to write one hundred lines."

"Please, Mrs. Scott, I didn't hurt her."

"Get busy and start writing. You cannot play outside until you finish."

My heart was broken, not because I had to write but because Mrs. Scott didn't believe me. She was punishing me for something I hadn't done. Martha and I both knew that, but I spent many recesses in tears, writing sentences. When finally finished, I no longer trusted Mrs. Scott.

She hurt me in much the same way my father hurt me. No, she didn't hit me, but I recall the lines on the paper. Each line I wrote felt like a slap on the face, a slap for something I didn't do.

Perhaps that is why, months later, when an older boy coerced me into the back shed at school, I didn't reveal the secret to her. "If you tell anyone I touched you, I will say it was your fault." I believed him and obediently followed him into the shed each time he had the opportunity to catch me alone. I dreaded school and dreaded recess even more.

When snow fell that year, I found my escape. Every recess we crossed the old dirt road and took to the small hills just across from the school. I used these recess opportunities to bundle up and slide down the hill on whatever I could use for a sled. Although he tried, he did not catch me alone again until spring.

Spring arrived, and the moment finally came when he caught me off guard and I found myself in the shed once again. But this time, I found the courage to speak. A winter in the hills had given me the confidence to not only speak but to speak boldly. "Go ahead. Tell Mrs. Scott. You can tell her anything you want. She will send me home, and I won't have to hide from you. Go. Tell."

He walked away and never told anyone. I marveled at the courage I had found from deep within. There was no way I could find that courage with my father, but that day, a victory had been won. I continued to be alert to the older boy's every move, but he no longer tried to catch me or molest me. His secret became my secret as well. It stayed hidden in a deep dark corner of my heart until much later in life.

I went to church from the time I was little because I had no choice. However, I went to Sunday school because I loved to go. Although my father bribed me with yummy pink peppermint candies, I couldn't sit still in church. My legs jumped and twitched. They would not cooperate no matter how hard I squeezed to keep them still. My father would allow it just so long and then out the backdoor I went. After some stern prompting, I returned, determined to sit quietly.

But in Sunday school, I was not under his scrutiny and could listen to stories, sing songs, and learn Bible verses while my legs kept moving. My teachers were not as concerned with my wiggling as with the verses I memorized. I soaked up God's Word like a sponge, even though I seldom understood what the verses meant. The one verse that I always remembered but my heart could not grasp was Ephesians 1:4 (NLT): "Even before he made the world, God loved us and chose us in Christ to be holy and without fault in his eyes."

My tender heart only absorbed the fact that even before he made the world, God loved me and chose me. I had no way to comprehend or understand what that love looked like. I could only base love on what I experienced from my earthly father, and I desperately tried to hide from his definition of love.

I vividly recall the weekends we spent at the cottage, swimming, waterskiing, and tubing. They were not only fun, they were my safe haven. I saw a side of my dad that I had never known. He pulled us around the lake behind the boat, trying his best to flip us into the water. When we finally fell, he was back to pick us up and drag us into the boat. We laughed and screamed, trying every trick we thought possible on water skis or on a tube. On Friday night when we arrived, the first thing Dad did was check the boat. He knew his twin brother would be arriving shortly and if the boat didn't run he was prepared to drive to Illinois to pick up my uncle's boat. After all, he didn't want us to miss a day of fun.

The cottage itself also gave me a glimpse of a different man. Building it was a huge undertaking. Preparation meant hauling sand, burning poison ivy, and bringing in lumber. We were involved in the work as much as possible, but the bulk of it fell on Dad's shoulders. It took one summer to put a roof over our heads, even if there were only studs with no walls and a simple kitchen and bathroom. We could live that way because Dad had to be available if we were going to be out on the lake.

On afternoons when Dad was working, I would swim across the lake, with Dennis close beside in the rowboat. We always waited until later in the day to avoid the endless line of speedboats pulling water skiers. Swimming the lake was a challenge I faced enthusiastically, knowing how much it impressed the neighborhood boys.

As much as I loved the thrill of swimming, waterskiing, and tubing, and as much as I loved swimming across the lake and back, the challenge of sailing the *Sunfish Sailboat* had to be my greatest joy. I could sail anytime I chose as long as someone knew I was on the lake. The wind determined the direction I would go, not the driver of a boat.

Each weekend, we arrived at the cottage on Friday evening, and late Saturday evening or early Sunday morning, we made the drive home just in time for church and the reality of another week. I delighted in the weekends so much that sometimes I forgot how much I dreaded the weekdays. Try to be good, try to be quiet, and most importantly, stay out of the way. My life was a roller-coaster ride, and there was no way to get off.

At the beginning of eighth grade, the little school I attended annexed with a larger neighboring school district. After close scrutiny, the school board found that for almost two years, our classwork had consisted of reading books and writing book reports. At semester break, the board deemed it necessary for the three eighth graders affected by this lack of curriculum to be placed in one of the district's elementary schools. This change meant I was attending a much larger school, meeting many new classmates, and doubling up in two curriculum areas—math and history.

Within a week, the classwork left me drowning in studies and staying up late at night to have homework completed for the following day. My mother helped as much as she could, but one in the morning usually arrived before I finished and went to bed. When test days dawned, my fingernails were bitten to the skin and tears lay waiting to burst at any moment. If my test grades were not what I expected, the tears fell freely.

The need to be perfect overpowered all sense of reasoning. I tried so hard to be perfect at home, hoping to avoid my father's anger, and I studied diligently in order to get perfect grades. Perfectionism didn't begin to solve the rejection and insecurity I felt. Late-night studies only succeeded in keeping me in turmoil and believing that I was dumb.

Studying so diligently and getting less-than-perfect grades did not compare to the constant teasing by the girls. My feet turned in, and the girls decided to taunt me by giving me a new name. "Pigeon-toed. She's pigeon-toed."

"My name is Lindsey, not pigeon-toed. I was born with my feet like this."

"We don't care. We're going to call you pigeon-toed. It is perfect."

"Please call me by my real name. Please." I could have told an adult, but the voice inside said, "They won't listen anyway." The girls seemed to know I wouldn't tell anyone, and it didn't take long before I isolated from them and started meeting the boys at recess to play. They didn't care whether my feet turned in as long as I could dunk a basketball and hit a softball.

After weeks of teasing, I finally found the courage to ask my mom. "Why didn't you have surgery on my legs so my feet would be straight? You don't know what it is like to be teased all the time."

"I was afraid you wouldn't be able to walk if we agreed to surgery. The doctor didn't know if your legs and feet would be straight, and I didn't want you to suffer."

I was close to finishing eighth grade, and I imagined the fear that had been a part of my mother's life. She had grown up in a home filled with superstition and fear. That fear had deprived me of the corrective surgery I needed when I was a tiny baby. Although God's word tells us in II Timothy 1:7, "God has not given us a spirit of fear and timidity, but of power, of love, and of a sound mind," we were both living in fear. Would that cycle of fear ever be broken?

Courage

I grew up having head knowledge about God but never knowing Him personally. Early in my high school years, I was invited to a Youth for Christ rally. It was there that someone tapped me on the shoulder and asked if I would like to go forward to accept Christ into my life. I began to cry as pent-up emotions surfaced, and the acknowledgement of sin in my life became a reality. That night, I made the decision to turn my life over to Christ.

That wasn't the end of my heartache, but it gave me a new purpose in life. I began to attend Youth for Christ meetings every Saturday night and soon was leading Youth for Christ meetings at school. I didn't have a lot of friends because I wanted my home life hidden, but at school, I had meetings to attend and a new desire to lead my peers to Christ.

It was at one of the Saturday meetings that I met my first boy-friend. Ron was older, but for some reason, my parents allowed me to see him if we were in a group setting or going to a Youth for Christ meeting. My heart ached for love, and Ron gave me the attention I desired and the bond between us grew. Not only did he give me the attention I desired, he began to point me in a direction that brought me closer to God.

Many times, we stayed at the house and talked, played board games, or took long walks. At Youth for Christ meetings, we were immersed in serving others. After months of seeing each other like this, I received an unusual phone call from Ron.

"Do you think your parent's will let me take you to see *The Sound of Music*?"

"I think you know the answer to that question. We have never gone anywhere unsupervised, and you know how my dad feels about movies. Never in a million years will he let me go."

"It wouldn't hurt to ask. You never know."

"I know that we will be home way past my curfew, and movies, well, they are out of the question according to my dad."

Ron was determined and soon convinced me that asking my mom first would be the best option. Although he knew nothing of my dad's wrath, he knew that I was fearful. Dad had changed, but I still had no reason to trust him.

It wasn't long before *The Sound of Music* arrived in local theaters. I had to ask now or skip the movie altogether. I didn't want to do that and finally mustered up enough courage to approach my mother.

"*The Sound of Music* is coming to local theaters in just a few weeks. I have never been to a movie, let alone a theater, and Ron wants to take me. I know it is past any curfew I might have, but please, do you think just this once we could go?"

"No. Not unless I talk to your father first. You know how he feels about movies."

"Yes, the same way he feels about homework on a Sunday afternoon. It is out of the question. But Mom, I do so want to go. *The Sound of Music* is a movie that families can attend together. Please."

"We both could get into real trouble if I give you permission to go and he finds out. I'm not sure I want you to risk that."

My mom was relentless, but so was I. It wasn't often that I was so determined, but after much convincing, she finally agreed to allow us to go to the theater. She actually taught me how to sneak in without getting caught.

"Make sure you take off your shoes and don't let the door slam. Be very quiet as you enter the house and tiptoe to your room."

"I will. I promise. But who will unlock the door? I don't have a key."

"You do now," she said as she handed me the key. "Be very careful when you put it in the lock and turn it."

"Who taught you how to sneak in at night? Was it your mother?"

"Yes, it was. If it had been for my dad, I think I would still be single."

"Thank you. I won't forget this." That night was special in more than one way. I had a new respect for my mother, and I went to a theater for the very first time. The movie was everything the advertisements portrayed, but the thought of returning home was constantly in my mind. Could I sneak in without getting caught, and if I did get caught, what would happen? One thing I knew for certain was I would never tell that Mom had helped me or given me the approval to go. I would never betray her.

The movie theater, which had been such a mystery, was now a reality. "I actually went to a movie and sat on the edge of my seat the entire movie. My legs started jumping only once. That's a miracle," I told Ron.

"It will be a miracle if we can get you in the house without getting caught. And yes, I enjoyed the movie very much, but I enjoyed watching you even more. Your eyes were glued to the screen. It's difficult to believe you have never been to a theater."

"You heard my mother. I'm surprised she allowed me to go this once. I've never asked before, assuming my father would say no. I guess I asked the right person. Now we'll see if I can get in without being caught."

Ron had parked down the street, and as soon as he gave me a quick kiss, he turned and started walking. I quietly unlocked the door, fumbling for a moment as I remembered the flashlight in my purse. It would light the way as I took my shoes off and unlocked the door. It would also guide me through the dark house and up to my room.

I turned the last corner in the hallway and almost jumped out of my skin. In the middle of the hallway, I saw this shadow, a shadow of a person I would not soon forget. Before I could open my mouth to scream, I heard this whisper.

"Be quiet. It's just me. Don't wake up your father."

"What are you doing up so late?"

"I wanted to make sure you got in, but more importantly, I wanted to hear about the movie. I didn't think I could wait until tomorrow, but now that you are home, it would probably be less of a risk if we talk tomorrow. Did you have fun?"

"The movie was breathtaking. The music, the scenery, and the Von Trapp family; it was all simply extraordinary. I will tell you about it tomorrow. Thanks, Mom, and good night."

We did talk the next day. Her cheeks flushed with excitement as she listened to every detail of *The Sound of Music*.

I dreamed about that evening for weeks to come even as I prepared to leave on a mission trip that would take me to Edmonton, Alberta, Canada. God had prepared this opportunity and I, along with three other teens, would be spending the summer counseling at different church camps and supervising and teaching children in various Bible schools.

My Choice

lthough my high school sweetheart and I had made a mutual
decision to go our separate ways, I wasn't going to let it put
a damper on what lay ahead. Quivering on the inside and
grinning on the outside, I drove the twenty minutes to Grand Valley
State University. The old brown Bel Air had four enormous doors
and cloth seats that showed wear and tear, but it was as dependable
as thunder following lightning.

The stretch of country road to the university always had a variety of crops, and this time of year, they were golden and ready for
harvest. The wind blowing through the open windows caused papers
I hadn't secured to blow throughout the car. I couldn't help but
laugh, even though I had to stop and find the wind-tossed papers.
My first day of college lay ahead, and I anticipated a freedom I had
never enjoyed. Yes, I had goosebumps on my arms and butterflies in
my stomach; but I was finally independent and looking forward to
days that would be filled with school, studies, and work. I struggled
to find my classes, and while wandering around campus, I found the
Youth for Christ sign. My heart skipped a beat. Now I knew this was
exactly where I wanted to be. Youth for Christ got me through high
school and it would be a constant in college.

Involvement in the Youth for Christ ministry meant helping the team remodel an old building, making it suitable for a coffeehouse. It had two floors with a railing full of potential slivers. It didn't matter. We still ran up and down those old stairs, not minding the tweezers and needles that followed. I loved the remodeling. My hands wrestled with the wood as we nailed window trim and floor boards in place. The warm and inviting ambiance seemed to attract high school and college students from all over Kent County. They came to talk about everything and anything. I had opportunities to share Christ, and when they accepted Jesus as their Savior, I asked myself, "Now what do I do?" They were new Christians and all I could say was, "Read your Bible."

The size of the old Bel Air made it perfect for carrying passengers to the coffeehouse. On one of those trips, a friend asked, "Would you like to go to a Navigator Bible Study?" I had heard the name of this organization mentioned before and I knew the guys would go.

Without giving it a thought, I agreed. That night, I learned about discipleship. I knew Jesus as my Savior and could share Him with others, but here was the missing piece, the piece that would help others grow in Christ. I listened with intent and decided I would go to the meeting again, with or without the others.

I didn't have to go alone. The following week, the car overflowed as we meandered our way to the downtown Navigator meeting. The speaker talked about discipleship again. In Matthew 28:19a, Jesus said, "Go therefore and make disciples of all nations." He explained how to become a disciple, a follower of Jesus. "It isn't just about making a decision; it's about a relationship with God."

As the Navigator study leaders were teaching me what it meant to follow Jesus, to surrender to Him, my eyes wandered around the room looking for someone to love me. Christ didn't seem to be enough. I desired to hear the words "I love you." I longed for physical touch. In fact, I chased after any man who so much as looked my way.

I searched the room during the next meeting and caught a glimpse of a man sitting in the opposite corner. He appeared to be a little older, but that did not hinder me. I inquired and quickly found out that his name was Ted. Three things drew me to him: he looked great, he had a nice car, and he hung around with the Navigators. I would make sure to open a window of opportunity. In opening that window, I took my eyes off God and placed them on a man.

This left me very vulnerable to what did not belong to me. Chasing men had caused struggles in the past. What made me think it would be any different now? Yet I followed after him. "He is a Christian, involved in ministry. He is everything I could ever desire."

My father said, "Slow down. If he is the man for you, it will happen in due time."

"No, Dad, he is perfect. I am going to date him. You'll see."

I wanted to be loved so badly, and when he finally started paying attention to me, I was ecstatic. As we dated, there were signs that raised red flags. Ted arrived late for every date, not just five minutes late but often a half-hour late. In my opinion, he spent way too much time with his parents and depended on them for everything. Somehow, I knew I could fix those things if we ever got married. I never dreamed that after dating six months I would be asked to make a decision that would shape who I am today.

On Christmas Eve, he arrived on time, grinning from ear to ear. Instead of coming in, he wanted me to come out to the car and open my Christmas present. Someone had wrapped the package so beautifully I didn't want to open it. "Open it now. I don't want you to wait."

"Can't I wait until tomorrow morning? It's not Christmas yet."

"No. Please open it tonight."

I finally agreed and began unwrapping it very carefully, not wanting to destroy the beautiful bow.

"Hurry," he said. "I can't wait."

When the wrapping fell away, I discovered a beautiful jewelry box.

"Keep going. There's more. Open it."

Inside the jewelry box, I found a very simple but very large diamond ring. My jaw must have dropped a foot.

"Will you marry me?"

We all make choices, but in the end our choices make us, and red flags or not, I answered yes.

Who wouldn't? My knight in shining armor, my hero, had just asked me to marry him. I had no clue as to the true definition of love, but I knew he was the man for me.

I didn't consult God. I just said yes.

"Let's elope," he said. "This week."

"But I want a church wedding. Let's wait until June."

"Can't we go someplace quiet and get married? We could be married by tomorrow evening."

I held my ground. I wanted time and a real wedding. It had been a childhood dream. After more discussion, Ted agreed to a June wedding. I had six months to finish another semester of school, to work, and plan a wedding. We still found time to stay involved with the Navigators. Involvement in ministry was the one bond that kept us strong.

During those six months, the red flags remained evident, but I didn't heed them. Ted was very close to his parents, working side by side with them in a family-owned carpet distribution business. His habit of being late caused dissension between my father and me. He saw the routine of being late as an indication of irresponsibility. Often, he would bet me a quarter as to the lateness of Ted's arrival. He always won and never minced words when he said, "Are you sure you want to live like this?"

"Dad, once and for all, I am sure. He is the man for me."

I didn't like the fact that he was late all the time, but I had learned early in my life to keep as quiet as possible. Words left unspoken seemed a wise choice. I somehow believed that his late arrivals would change once we were married.

With red flags buried inside, I continued to complete wedding plans and finish school. I also designed and created the dresses for my wedding party. The peach hues, the empire waistlines, and the flowing hemlines combined together, creating an exquisite dress. My dress had the same empire waistline, but I covered it with lace and attached a train that trailed behind me forever. I designed and tailored these dresses for royalty because we were each God's chosen bride, His royalty.

School was finished, and our wedding plans were complete. We had one week left to spare, allowing us just enough time to reflect on the past six months and look toward our future. A Cinderella wedding with the bride and groom living happily ever after is probably every little girl's dream, and mine was no exception.

The last week before the wedding, we designated our week. The week had only begun when Ted announced, "I have to go out of town on business for three days but will return with plenty of time for the rehearsal."

"Do you really have to go this week? We were supposed to spend time finishing preparations for the wedding."

"You said preparations for the wedding were complete and this is important. I have to go."

I knew the subject was closed and convinced myself that he was right. He had to go. I kept busy finishing last-minute details, but when rehearsal time came and the hands on the clock began to tick slower and slower, I must admit I had my doubts.

When the church door finally opened and the groom appeared, my body relaxed; my worry and anxiousness subsided. I quickly made up an excuse. "He is always this late," I said.

My dad eased the tension. "Let's get the rehearsal going. The food is still hot, and I am hungry."

The rehearsal didn't go as smoothly as I would have liked, especially after the stress related to the late start. The maid of honor came in on the wrong cue, the children didn't want to be on stage, and my dad appeared with a frown on his face. As we walked down the aisle, his words echoed in my ears. "Is this how you want to spend the rest of your life?"

After everyone left, Ted and I talked briefly about the evening.

"I had every intention of being on time. Did you think I wouldn't show up?"

"I didn't know what to think. It did cross my mind that you weren't going to show. I also wondered if you had an accident."

"Well, I wasn't that late."

"Thirty minutes is late, and it was our wedding rehearsal. I don't understand why you had to be late at all."

"I am sorry. Time slipped away."

When he dropped me off, tension filled the night air around us. "Tomorrow is our wedding. Let's be happy." He hugged and kissed me before he left me at the door. Unspoken were the words I wanted to say. Instead, I shrugged my shoulders and unlocked the door to the house.

I went to bed almost immediately, but sleep evaded me. I struggled with the memories of the evening and the future that lay ahead.

Morning finally arrived, and all the plans and preparation of the past six months finally came to fruition. My bridesmaids chatted incessantly as they dressed and made sure their hair was just right. I quietly did the same thing. And as I looked at myself in the mirror, I asked, "Are you sure this is what you want for the rest of your life?"

The moment came when I put all fear aside, linked my arm in my father's arm, and followed my bridal party down the aisle. All eyes were on me, the bride to be. As I approached the altar, my eyes caught Ted's eyes, and all was right with the world. We repeated our vows. He kissed me, and almost before it began, the wedding was over. As we turned to the crowd, Pastor Van introduced us.

"I present to you Mr. and Mrs. Ted Jonson."

Our Honeymoon

We could have spent our honeymoon in a fancy resort but instead decided to spend two weeks at his parent's cabin in Northern Michigan. The smell of the pine wood interior, the huge fireplace that glowed as the embers died down, and the river down below the bank made it a perfect place to begin our lives together. As he drove, I reflected on the previous day, not certain as to how the past six months had passed so quickly. I mumbled the words out loud, "Mrs. Lindsey Jonson, Mrs. Lindsey Jonson."

The warmth of the day and the sun shining in the windows made me sleepy. I dozed off, and when Ted finally woke me, we were approaching the narrow dirt lane that would take us back to the cabin. He said, "This is where my family loves to be when life is falling apart."

I replied, "What about when life is calm and serene?"

There was no answer. My mind began to ponder what he said, but I quickly dismissed it as he unlocked the door and carried me over the threshold. He chose the room we would call our own for the next two weeks, and as we unpacked, the intimacy of the moment unfolded. Ted had chosen me to be his bride, and nothing else mattered.

We went fishing and hiking. We laid in the living room where we could see the sunset.

We fought off the mosquitoes, which were famous in the northern woods. We played with the dogs and talked about the future. For a brief amount of time, our lives began to mesh.

After five days of wedded bliss and an early morning cup of coffee, we were both startled to hear the phone ring. He answered, but I could hear his father very clearly. "Your grandmother just passed away. You have to come home."

We packed very little and drove home in silence. Ted wanted to get there as soon as possible. He had lost a loved one and wanted to be with his family. As soon as we entered the house, it became evident that I would not be included in their grieving. I happened to be the outsider, the newest member of the family, and possibly unintentionally, they excluded me.

When we left the cemetery, Ted's father announced that the entire family would be accompanying us to the cabin for the final days of our honeymoon. I stared at Ted in dismay. He looked back at me and said, "That's the way it is. We are family."

We were the first ones to arrive. Ted started a fire to take the chill from the cabin.

When my sister-in-law and her family arrived, she looked around and announced, "You're sleeping in our bedroom." Visibly angry, she lashed out at me as if I had done something wrong.

Ted said nothing. Instead, he packed our things to move to another room. The honeymoon was definitely over as the attacks continued. No matter what I did, I did it wrong. And then I remembered Ted's words, "This is where my family comes when everything seems to be falling apart." Things were definitely falling apart.

We stayed at the cabin with his family for one week. Although his family treated me harshly, Ted and I still had fun fishing and walking in the river. I stayed away from the cabin as much as possible, and when the time arrived for us to return to our new home, I thought I could finally relax.

Leave and Cleave

Genesis 2:24 tells us, "Therefore a man leaves his father and his mother and clings to his wife, and they become one flesh." That didn't happen in the Jonson household. When Ted wasn't traveling, he spent a portion of every morning at his parents', discussing business and listening to them belittle me. He did not miss the opportunity to return home to repeat their words, negative words that pierced to the very deepest parts of my heart. "You are not a good wife and you do not support me in my work," were just a few of the phrases I heard so often.

Soon, I began to believe those words. Triggers from my past exploded, and I began to act on the words. I cried and nagged, "Please don't go there, and do not repeat what they say." No longer were my words kind. Instead, they were demanding. I desired love and instead suffered rejection. My heart ached to the core.

I finally talked to my mother. She very wisely said, "You must forgive."

"I just can't seem to forgive, Mom. This happens daily."

Her response, "God calls you to forgive, but that doesn't mean you will forget."

"Thanks, Mom, I will try."

The words spoken were so damaging, but the lack of physical touch that had been a part of our relationship prior to marriage hurt even more. His desire for intimacy had dissipated, and my hormones were raging. Although I dressed for success, I learned very quickly that our bedroom would be a place of rejection. I cried, begged, and pleaded, but to no avail. He wanted to sleep. "Something is wrong with you," he said. And I believed him.

"It is not a lack of love, but a lack of friendship that makes unhappy marriages," Friedrich Nietzsche said.

The Navigator ministry was our one common ground. We never missed a study and often were involved in the ministry. We both were excited to see people come to know Jesus as their Savior and just as excited to watch them grow. But we failed to talk about what was important in each of our lives. We had no clue as to likes and dislikes. How I hid what my heart was feeling, I will never know.

Ted loved golf and played as often as possible during the week. Every weekend, he went to the golf course as well, and he was good—tournament good. I knew nothing about golf and tried to learn but seemed to be the flaw in the midst of his game. I heard him say repeatedly, "You have to take this seriously. It's not about fun but about winning the game."

I replied just as often, "I can follow the rules, but I cannot hit the ball. I just want to have fun."

I caddied once in a while, but more often than not, I spent the weekends alone. I loved water skiing, swimming, and sailing, but I did not want to go to the cottage alone. I could easily have picked up the keys to my car, but I could hear my dad say, "Who wears the pants in your house?" That was the last thing I needed, and so I stayed home.

During our first year of marriage, I finished college and received my teaching certificate. In the middle of turmoil, I persevered. Although I didn't enjoy my college classes, I knew I needed to get my degree. No longer did I drive the old brown Bel Air to school. A fancy sports car replaced it. I didn't care. A sports car was not what I desired. I wanted love and intimacy.

A breakthrough, if nothing else, an opportunity for our marriage to prevail, surfaced after one year. Ted's parents wanted him to move to another location in Michigan, and I found a teaching position in the same area. *This must be the answer to leave and cleave*, I thought. Ted would certainly be more present if we were not so close to his parents.

I had developed a deep resentment towards Ted and his parents during our first year of marriage. The thought of being away from them caused me to have hope. Resentment was causing me to say "I hate you" far too often. It was never said aloud, but God doesn't make a distinction about that in His Word. We are commanded not to hate our brother.

Change of location does not change circumstances, and it did not change ours. Ted just traveled more and spent equally as much time with his parents. The only difference was that since he was on the road, he didn't come home every day to give me information as to my status as a wife, and this caused some of the resentment to lift.

Our new location gave me the opportunity to teach at a school for the first time. It wasn't an easy year. I taught thirty-five students in a portable unit designed for twenty-seven, and if that didn't make for chaos, wasps dive-bombing in the room certainly did. But God had given me the gift of teaching, and I loved it. I not only taught at school but also had the opportunity to minister to many teenage girls. Being used by God comforted me, and although my marriage hadn't changed, this part of my life provided a source of deep contentment.

This contentment lasted a little more than one year before I found myself getting ready to move back to the other side of Michigan. A phone call from Ted's parents left no room for discussion. "We need you closer for business." I was devastated as I said goodbye to my teaching job and to a hope forming inside.

I cried as I said "I love you" to the girls I had been spending so much time with. I had been down dark paths, but the future seemed even darker. I was so thankful I could drive back to Grand Rapids in my own car. The time alone gave me the opportunity to pray and meditate. I couldn't help but wonder if God did have a plan for my life.

Driving back to Grand Rapids, unpacking the truck, and facing his parents left me totally overwhelmed. Without so much as a thought, Ted announced, "I'm leaving but will be back shortly to help unpack." I knew that statement didn't hold water, but I remained silent.

When he returned, it was much later, and he had conveniently missed the unpacking for the day. His habit of showing up late hadn't changed. As he walked through the door, I said "good night" rather curtly and headed for the chaos in the bedroom. We had to be able to sleep.

Although I wasn't teaching, I seemed more at peace after the move. I couldn't change Ted's behavior, but I could go to church and we were once again involved with the Navigators. I thought the turmoil in our marriage was a secret, but it was not long until our Navigator ministry team leader and his wife asked to meet for coffee. He looked directly at me. "What is troubling you? Something is causing unrest, and I would like to help."

"There is nothing you can do to help. I am fine. I have been balancing marriage, teaching, and ministry, and it's not easy."

"The team has discussed it, and we believe it is time for both of you to take a break. We want you to come to the Discipleship Study, but we think it is time for you to focus on you. We'll talk to Ted but wanted to hear what you had to say first."

"Please, isn't there something I can do to help?"

"No, there isn't. This is not all about you, Lindsey. Ted is involved as well. We will talk to him next."

By now, I had been programmed to believe it was all my fault. I knew it was all about me. I wanted to tell them what happened in our home behind closed doors, but I had kept quiet for so long. I wasn't about to air my dirty laundry now.

Why am I staying in this marriage? I asked myself. *Is this the way it's supposed to be?* My answer was always the same. *I am staying for God and for the ministry. There are no other options.* But now, the Navigator ministry was being stripped from me.

As our relationship spun into a downward spiral, I began to consider the options I didn't think were there. I could leave if I chose to, at least for a short time. That would give me time to regroup and to pray away from the line of fire. But I had read the Bible and thought the answer was rock solid. I could not leave for long. I had to return.

I waited at least one month and then packed a small suitcase and journeyed to a place of solitude and safety. A friend recognized the underlying signs and said, "If you ever need a place to go, you are welcome here." I left town that day knowing that I would return, just not knowing when.

I could hear my father say, "You're wrong. You must submit to his authority." But I also remembered very vividly the way my father treated me, and there was something wrong with that picture as well.

Could his interpretation of submission be skewed?

I spent four weeks wondering what my future held. I knew Proverbs 16:3, "Commit your work to The Lord, and your plans will be established." I had committed my work to God, but I certainly didn't see his plan for my life. I didn't communicate with anyone during my time away and rather focused on God and healing. I basked in the sun and enjoyed the peace and quiet.

When the four weeks were coming to a close, I made the decision to return to my husband. I feared what I would encounter at home, but believed I had to go back. I repacked my suitcase slowly and deliberately. I waited until my friend returned before I left. "Thank you for your kindness and love. Your vacation home has been a safe haven, and I will be forever grateful."

"You don't have to go. My home is open to you day or night. Are you sure?"

"I don't have a choice. I have to go."

I drove slowly, knowing that I faced a man who seemed to love his family and golf even more than his wife. I drove home knowing that I had not kept contact for a month. A mutual friend had called him saying, "She is safe." That had been my only contact.

When I arrived at the house, his golf clubs were not in their usual spot. I knew exactly where he was. It didn't take long for me to realize that his absence was a blessing in disguise. I unpacked and walked around the house. *I should not have returned. I can still leave while I have the chance.* Just then, the door opened and Ted entered. His return made the decision for me. I couldn't leave now; I couldn't leave ever.

I waited for him to say something, anything. After a long silence, he said, "I just played 18 holes of golf and shot a 5 under par. That is pretty good, don't you think?"

I wanted to hit him, just to see if I could get a reaction from him. *Did he only think about golf? Will this ever end?* I had disappeared for one month, and he hadn't noticed I was missing? At that point, I did not know whether to laugh or cry. I started to leave the room, but Ted took my arm and pulled me close. We embraced, and then he gently led me to the bedroom.

"I missed you. I didn't know if you were coming back."

"I made the decision earlier this week and almost changed my mind today. You came home shortly after I arrived, and your arrival made the decision."

To hear Ted say he missed me and then seem to take an interest in me intimately was quite a surprise, a pleasant surprise. I had adjusted to his mediocre interest in physical touch, but when he desired me, dressed for success or not, I was eager. Possibly, my absence had triggered something inside.

Heartache

It wasn't long after one of those rendezvous that I began to wake up in the morning sick to my stomach. When this continued, I made an appointment with Dr. Post, my ob-gyn. He was like the father I always wanted. Gentleness and kindness were always on his doorstep. If he could be described in one word, it would be compassionate.

After doing a thorough exam, he turned to me and said, "You are pregnant." I didn't know whether to laugh or cry. It had only been three months since I had made the decision to return home. I counted the days on my fingers and knew exactly the night I conceived. Even though I was eager for intimacy, that night felt like a one-night stand. Ted had rushed, not thinking of my needs.

As I was getting ready to leave the office, many thoughts were running through my mind. These thoughts tumbled out. *What will Ted think? Maybe a baby will help our marriage.*

I stopped short when I heard Dr. Post say one more thing. "We haven't talked about this, but it's no secret with me. You need to start eating now rather than later."

I mumbled, "Yes," and then asked, "How did you know?"

"How did I know what? That you do not eat enough? It's easy, Lindsey. You hide it well, but you are very thin and very close to, if not, anorexia."

"I am not anorexic. I am not!"

"I am not going to argue with you. I know that won't work. But you are eating for two now. I will be monitoring you closely, and if I don't see improvement in your weight, I will be forced to get the help you may need."

That is just what I needed right now. I didn't stop to ask if he meant a psychiatrist or a dietician. I simply knew I needed to make the choice to eat.

I arrived home with plenty of time to make a nice dinner. When Ted stepped in the, door it was waiting, cold, but still waiting. When he finished eating, I blurted out the words, "I am pregnant."

Ted was full of questions. "You are? You are actually pregnant? That is terrific! When?"

"I don't know the answer to that question, but I think I know the night I conceived. I am so glad you are happy. I didn't know if you would be."

We talked a little about the baby, and then exhaustion pushed me to the bedroom. I needed a good night's sleep. There was no way to predict the days that lay ahead. I was sick every day, all day. Throughout the entire pregnancy, I was in and out of the hospital. Each time Dr. Post assured us, "The baby will be fine."

After one of these trips to the hospital, Ted said, "I thought they called this morning sickness."

I replied, "Believe me, I thought so too, but for me it's all-day sick."

I tried to eat. Some days a little of the food I actually ate did stay down. It was a miracle that I did start to gain weight. As the months progressed, I finally felt the baby move, and a few days later, Ted felt the baby move too. He once again surprised me when he said, "Before now, the bump in your stomach just seemed like something that made you sick. Now I know there is a baby." As his fingers lingered on my stomach, he fell asleep. At that moment, I knew this child was going to be what the doctor ordered to heal our marriage.

It wasn't easy, but God was teaching me patience and forgiveness as I carried this precious bundle during a very long nine months. Ted seemed more interested in being home and tried desperately to help when I was so sick. Memories of what my mother had said about forgiveness were fresh in my mind, and Matthew 6:15 was a constant reminder. "But if you do not forgive others their sins, your Father will not forgive your sins."

As the due date drew closer, my friends began to decorate the baby's room. We decided to paint the room pale yellow and add accent colors of pink or blue after the baby was born. The dresser drawers were beginning to fill.

Ted and I began to talk about what would happen if I went into labor while he was traveling. The stubborn part of me said *I'll drive myself to the hospital*. We talked about other options, and fortunately, the other options did not include his family.

All the planning didn't make any difference the night I began to experience very sharp stomach pains. I had never felt labor pains but couldn't imagine them being this intense. Ted was home and finally called the emergency room.

After explaining the circumstances, he asked. "Should I bring her in?"

The emergency room staff said, "It's your call. We don't know what is happening, so it is up to you to make that decision."

He responded, "We are on our way."

Ted raced in and out of traffic. I was amazed at how quickly we arrived at the emergency room. The pain came and went while I was in the car, and I began to think we should have stayed home.

There was no waiting when we arrived at the hospital. I was immediately taken to an emergency room. I told the doctor in charge, "I'm feeling better."

He said, "I will determine that." And he proceeded to get my vitals. The look of alarm in his eyes while he was taking my blood pressure indicated that I might not be fine.

He quickly made me lie flat and then said, "Please stay that way until you are told differently." He left and returned with another doctor. "We will begin running tests as soon as the room is ready. Until then, try to relax."

That request seemed easy for him to make but so much harder to follow. It appeared I did not understand the gravity of the situation, but one thing I knew for sure was that the sharp pains were not labor pains. They were something far more serious.

Dr. Post arrived shortly after I entered the examining room. A grim look replaced the usual smile. He talked to me for just a minute and then went to change. When he returned in his scrubs, he looked so calm and assured, but his eyes said something else. He talked very little as he began to examine me and prepare for an ultrasound.

During the ultrasound, everyone in the room remained quiet and reserved. No one gave us any information. As they rolled me back to the emergency room, I heard one of the interns say, "Admit her. Find a room and keep her flat on her back with her feet elevated."

Dr. Post walked in and began to explain what they had seen during the ultrasound. "The placenta has torn, and your blood pressure is way too high to operate. There is no doubt we would lose you during surgery." Then he added, "Right now, we can only hope and pray that your little boy stays alive long enough for your blood pressure to drop."

"Little boy," I cried. "Are you certain it's a boy?"

I didn't hear the answer. The IV the nurse had inserted in my arm earlier now carried prescribed medication into my blood stream. I slept for what seemed like hours.

For five days, I remained flat in bed, learning how to eat without raising my head.

Dr. Post checked me often and always heard my little boy's heartbeat. But he could only monitor me because my blood pressure would not budge.

Then late Sunday afternoon, he made a surprise visit. "Just wanted to check on my star patient," he said. "I was making my rounds and thought I would stop." He put his stethoscope on my stomach and held it far longer than he had done in the past. Then he took my blood pressure.

"I wish it would go down. You blood pressure has to come down in order for me to safely perform a C-section."

"What does this mean? Please tell me."

"I will be here first thing in the morning to check again. Right now, I can't hear a heartbeat, but that doesn't mean I will not hear it in the morning." I didn't ask any questions, rather closed my eyes and prayed. Soon, I was sleeping again.

As promised, Dr. Post arrived before sunup with his stethoscope in hand. He placed it on my stomach and listened very carefully. Finally, he said, "I still do not hear a heartbeat."

Again, I responded with the same question, "What does that mean?"

He chose his words very carefully. "That means I will check again later. It means the baby may be turned wrong or possibly, he may have died."

He held me as I began to sob. He tried to soothe me, knowing that my blood pressure was still elevated to a dangerous level. Finally, he told the nurse, "Please call her husband."

When Ted arrived, he followed him in the door. He explained what was happening and then said, "I still cannot operate. She will not survive surgery."

He left us alone and returned later to check for a heartbeat. This time, I pushed him away and said, "No, no more stethoscopes and no more listening. Our baby is dead."

He said, "You can't be so certain."

"Yes, I can," I cried. "I have total peace that he is in heaven."

He didn't question me more, nor did he check for a heartbeat again. Instead, he checked my blood pressure and noticed that it had dropped considerably. As he left, I heard him talking to the staff.

Within an hour, he returned to let us know that he would be inducing labor as soon as possible and hopefully the delivery would go smoothly and quickly. He must have read my mind.

"No C-section," he said. "I don't want to lose you now."

I heard the words clearly. They are going to induce labor. It shouldn't take too long for him to be born. If the time it took to prepare for labor was indicative of the time it would take to deliver the baby, then delivery would be an eternity away. I waited patiently, knowing that I could not begin healing until after I delivered the baby.

Very shortly after the Pitocin entered my system, the labor pains began. They were excruciating and all in my back. I cried silently.

"Please, God, help him come soon. I cannot bear this much longer." I bit my lips as I tried so hard not to scream. Pain medication delivered through the IV caused me to relax, and then the drugs to induce labor had to be delivered once again into the IV. It was a vicious cycle. Ted tried to reassure me, but he could not make the baby come. I had to do that alone. I had to endure the labor alone, and soon, I became too exhausted to even try. Under normal circumstances, a baby naturally helps with the birth, but a stillborn baby isn't normal and they do not help. They cannot say, "Get me out of here."

Finally, after almost forty-eight hours, I had dilated from one centimeter to six centimeters. "Just a little more," Dr. Post encouraged. "The baby is small and it's almost time." His strong arms wrapped around me, and I continued what seemed like a never-ending task.

But just like that, it was time. "Into the delivery room you go," he said. And within minutes, Luke was born.

Ted had been in and out of the labor room, but he did not go into the delivery room. After the birth of our baby, he returned to console me. Right then, I did not want to be consoled.

"Do you want to see Luke?" he asked.

"No. I don't want to see him. You take care of everything."

My pastor conducted a small funeral service for Luke the following day. I was too weak to go anywhere.

"Why didn't I see him? Why didn't they wait until I was strong enough to attend the funeral service?" These are questions that will only be answered in heaven.

I reflect on the birth of Luke, remembering the sorrow and grief that accompanied his birth. As time passed, I saw God's plan for him in a different light. Isaiah 55:8–9 speaks of what I have learned. "For my thoughts are not your thoughts, nor are your ways my ways, says the Lord. For as the heavens are higher than the earth, so are my ways higher than your ways and my thoughts than your thoughts."

I rejoice, knowing that Luke never endured pain or suffering on earth. He went to be with his Heavenly Father in a way much higher than my way.

Another

The death of our son strengthened our marriage. Ted didn't come home as often repeating the comments of his parents, and he paid more attention to my needs and wants. He touched and held me, and our relationship became more intimate.

Six months had gone by, and I still had not had a menstrual cycle. One morning, I woke up feeling nauseated. The next morning, I felt the same way. I waited one week and then called Dr. Post's office. The receptionist scheduled my appointment in two weeks. At the appointment, Dr. Post went through the regular routine of an unplanned checkup. When he finished, he said, "I need to take a urine specimen, but I am certain you are pregnant."

"There's no way," I cried. "I can't be pregnant again."

As always, Dr. Post responded in a gentle and reassuring tone of voice. "You are, and everything is fine. I know what you are thinking, but losing a second baby happens so seldom."

"But what if?" I said.

"No what if," he said. "Everything will be fine."

"Fine. It's only been six months since I delivered Luke. How can everything be fine?"

My voice began to quiver, and the tears welled up in my eyes as I added, "Ted doesn't seem to care about me until he wants something, and when he does, I end up pregnant." Memories of losing Luke still wreaked havoc with my emotions, and I didn't want to go through that again. I had no choice but to trust Dr. Post.

My instructions were to enjoy life, to eat, and to rest. Thankfully, my body handled this pregnancy in a different way, and I could actually eat without running to the bathroom every time. I did not want to be pregnant, but I repeated the Psalmist words, "Children are a gift of the Lord, the fruit of the womb is a gift." I couldn't understand this hesitation but later reasoned that the fear of losing another child must have masked the excitement that I felt over having another child.

I struggled through those early months, always playing the what-if game. Could it be that I did not totally trust God for the outcome of the child within me? The fear of losing another child hindered me from relaxing and enjoying the season that God had given me. As I entered my third month, I noticed some weight gain.

Eating enough continued to be a struggle, and gaining weight put me into a tailspin of sorts. "If he doesn't love me when I am thin, how will he love me when I am fat?" That continued to be the 100-dollar question, but when Dr. Post announced, "You have gained four pounds this month," I could not help but applaud with him. I had a new life inside me, and the baby needed those pounds.

Although Ted still traveled most weeks, I no longer whined and begged for him to stay home. Being on the road or at home wasn't the issue. Traveling on business with his family and the words of belittlement he brought home to me were the source of resentment and irritation. I didn't want to hear it. My self-esteem had been low prior to losing our son, and now I wasn't sure I could do anything right.

He wasn't home when I heard the baby's heartbeat for the first time, and he wasn't home when I felt the baby move ever so slightly. I lay in bed quietly that evening, waiting for it to happen one more time. It was the following day before the baby moved again, but when I felt that tiny kick, I squealed with delight. I praised God once again for this new life inside me and prayed for a healthy baby.

Shopping for maternity clothes, sewing little blankets and towels, and picking out baby clothes proved to be a source of delight. I had been too sick during my first pregnancy to enjoy preparing for a baby. Everyone else did it for me. I was beginning to believe what Dr. Post said, "You are going to be fine and so is that baby."

Ted had been on the road for four days, and when he arrived home, he offered me a wonderful surprise. "Do you think you can go on a business/golf trip with me to the Upper Peninsula?"

"I want to go very much," I exclaimed. "But I'll have to get approval from Dr. Post. It's important that I follow his directions."

"Go ahead and call him. I don't want to go against doctor's orders. And I want to have a child as much as you do."

This did not appear to be the same man I married. He was considering my feelings in the matter. I left the room to call the receptionist at the office. Could I really go? Would Dr. Post say it was all right?

I didn't expect him to say yes. I heard the word *no* so often that hearing it again would not have surprised me. Now I heard Dr. Post say, "You are almost five months along. Everything is fine. Go and have fun."

As I packed, my mind focused on the changes I had seen in Ted the last few months. "Maybe he was beginning to see the importance of leaving the attachment to his parents and working on our marriage instead. I could hardly contain myself as I packed for our four-day trip. I picked out a new maternity outfit from the closet. The navy slacks and the white and navy top would be perfect when we went out for dinner. The rest of the clothes were casual and sporty. Finally, I put in my Bible and a book about marriage. I would want them in the car while he was at the dealerships that regularly purchased carpet from him.

We left early the following day listening to music as he drove, switching stations when we lost reception. I felt relaxed and comfortable. He stopped for one business call while I read and slept. We drove just a little longer that first day and stopped in a quaint northern Michigan motel for the night. The quilt on the bed reminded me of the ones I made on a regular basis. The Log Cabin design suited the room perfectly. A quiet dinner consisting of a salad and shrimp kabobs followed by a short walk put me at ease. "Yes," I told myself. "This is just what the doctor ordered."

I slept like a log, waking up rested and eager to begin the day. Before breakfast, I took time to read my Bible and pray. I was encouraged as I read Philippians 4:6. "Don't fret or worry. Instead of worrying, pray. Let petitions and praises shape your worries into prayers, letting God know your concerns." I talked to God about my marriage, and this pregnancy. I did have concerns. Then I finished getting ready for breakfast. It still amazed me that I could eat without getting sick in the morning.

After breakfast, we took our time getting packed. Ted intended to stop for an early afternoon golf game at his favorite course. As expected, the grounds at the northern Michigan course were impeccable. Riding along in the cart while he played provided me with the opportunity to enjoy the fragrance of the freshly cut grass and see the breathtaking view of Lake Michigan this course provided. By the time we were finished, my arms and face had turned a golden brown.

He packed his clubs and took a quick shower. He still had to drive the rest of the way to Paradise, Michigan. Paradise is at the tip of the Upper Peninsula, and its high cliffs border Lake Superior. At that time, there were one or two places to stay and the same variety when it came to restaurants. The town consisted of 250 to 300 people. The sound of water splashing against the shoreline and the smell of water as it rose into the air made Paradise a perfect place to stay. Possibly, that is why they called it Paradise. The cabin we chose was within walking distance of the bluffs that bordered this portion of the lake. It was going to be a cool evening, so Ted put some wood in the fireplace and started a fire before we strolled out to view the lake.

As we walked back, I felt a strange sensation in my stomach. *My mind is playing tricks on me*, I said under my breath. I grabbed pajamas and went to get cleaned up. As I undressed and stepped into the shower, I noticed something red on the floor of the tub. I looked again and then reached down to feel it. It was blood, my blood. I screamed in disbelief. Ted came running, not knowing what was happening.

I knew from past experience that I needed to be off my feet, and that we had to call Dr. Post. His answering service picked up the call, and Ted left a message. One very long hour later, he confirmed what I already knew. "Stay off your feet and stay put. Traverse City is the closest hospital with a neonatal trauma center."

Paradise, Michigan, is a very lonely place when you are in crisis. Dr. Post's words echoed in my ears. "Everything will be fine. You will have a healthy baby." I wanted so desperately to believe that.

"How can you say that when I am spotting?" I cried. "I shouldn't be spotting."

Dr. Post continued to be encouraging. "It's just a little, and it most likely will stop. Try to rest."

But my heart was beginning to tell me something different. I continued to spot just a little even though I was following orders and staying off my feet. I found myself wanting to go to the bathroom just to see if the bleeding had stopped.

Dr. Post continued to be encouraging, repeating the same advice. "It's just a little and it most likely will stop. Try to rest."

After two days of living on pins and needles, Dr. Post finally made the decision. "It's time to get down to Munson Hospital in Traverse City. You're going to have to go tomorrow."

I had such high hopes, but reality was sinking in. "If I leave Paradise, I am giving up. As long as I stay here, the baby will be fine." But Dr. Post insisted that I had to get to the neonatal unit. I had trusted him before. I had to trust him again.

The decision was made to transport, and I asked the next question. "How do we get to the hospital?"

The ambulance service would only take me to the closest hospital, one without a neonatal center. Dr. Post said no.

The next possible option was Ted's parents. They were at their cabin and were driving their suburban. With the seats' back in a reclined position, I could lay down comfortably. The drive from the cabin to Paradise was not too long, and the trip back down to Traverse City was manageable. His parents agreed to be the transport.

As Ted carried me to the car, I wondered how I would stay calm riding with them for three and a half hours. The berating and belittling were always fresh in my mind. His parents seemed preoccupied, and that gave me time to lay in the back of the suburban and rest. Memories constantly invaded my mind, memories of losing Luke and the recent words of Dr. Post. "It won't happen again."

"God, I prayed. You have promised to be with me." In Psalm 30:5b, the Psalmist said, "Weeping stays for the night, but joy comes in the morning." There will be joy in the morning. I am going to have this baby. Dr. Post said that losing a child rarely happens twice.

I wept silently, not wanting my in-laws to know the anguish in my heart. Instinctively, I started singing Sunday school songs under my breath. The same songs rang over and over in my head. "Jesus Loves the Little Children," "This Little Light of Mine," and "Jesus Loves Me." Praising God lightened my heart and time passed quickly. I sat up just enough to see Lake Michigan in its entire splendor as we crossed the Mackinaw Bridge.

The bridge to the hospital in Traverse City isn't a long drive, and when I entered the hospital on a stretcher, Dr. Post wasn't there. I knew that would be the case, but I didn't realize how much I depended on him. My thoughts ran wild. He had been with me when I gave birth to Luke. How could I trust strangers? This was not at all what I had planned.

After the initial exam in the emergency room, the staff whisked me away to a very cold, very sterile neonatal room. I wanted lots and lots of blankets. My teeth were chattering, and I couldn't stop shaking. Ted met me in that cold room. He asked for even more blankets and wrapped them around me. He listened carefully as the doctor responded to his question. "How is my wife and how is the baby?"

"Right now, she is stable. We are going to do an ultrasound as soon as we can get her ready. We will know more about the baby then."

"If she is okay, I am going to grab a bite to eat with my parents and then I'll be back."

Ted was waiting in the room when I returned from the ultrasound. We both wanted answers, but no one returned with test results. The room was quiet, and I was trying very much to stay composed. We both jumped when the phone in the hospital room rang.

Ted answered it and then handed the phone to me. "It's Dr. Post, and he wants to talk to you."

"The doctor that is caring for you called." His voice cracked as he said, "They have the results of the ultrasound. The baby is no longer alive."

"No, they're wrong," I cried. "You promised, you promised." Although Dr. Post was far away, I could feel his presence beside me. I wanted to shake him, to tell him he had lied, but all I could do was listen as he tried to explain between my sobs. I wanted to get up and run, to escape this room and all that was happening around me. I kept saying, "You promised, you promised. You promised the baby would be fine and the baby is not fine. Our baby is dead."

The doctor at Munson Medical walked in shortly after I hung up the phone. Both Ted and the doctor tried to comfort me, but I wanted no part of it. "How can this be? How can our baby be dead?"

"I called your doctor because I wanted him to tell you. Stop and listen, please. Your baby is small, and Dr. Post and I agree that it is best if the baby comes naturally. It shouldn't take too long."

"Too long. You are telling me it will not take too long. That's what they said about our stillborn son. Now you are going to try to convince me the delivery will not take too long." Nothing could convince me. The delivery of Luke had taken forever.

I didn't have to wait long for the doctor to induce labor. Two or three hours after the Pitocin was added to my IV, another stillborn baby was delivered. The doctor in Traverse City was right about two things. My labor pains were minimal compared to those I had with Luke, and it didn't take long. I stayed awake after delivery just long enough to utter, "Another child is in heaven. This was not supposed to happen. Dr. Post promised."

Ted stepped out for a few minutes and returned with two yellow roses. They were on the nightstand when I woke up. "This doesn't make up for your loss, but I thought they might lift your spirits a little." The roses were not only looked beautiful, they also filled the room with a sweet-smelling fragrance.

I had to ask Ted where they took her and how our baby looked. He didn't give me much information. Maybe he did not want to upset me, but reflecting on those moments reminds me that he was grieving as well.

The circumstances that followed may have led me to believe he did not care. He left the room for a short time, and when he returned, he had good news. "What good news could you possibly have on such a tragic morning?" I said.

"We are going to the cabin for a week, so you will have time to rest and recuperate."

I looked at him in disbelief. "But your parents are there. I want to go home. Please take me home."

"We will only be there one week. It will give you time to rest, and I can play a little golf with my dad."

My mind centered on going home to grieve, and his mind focused on being with his parents. There were no words to express the sorrow and rejection I felt at that moment. I clung to the hospital bed, not wanting to let go. I had memorized Psalm 46:1, and I repeated it over and over. "God is my refuge and strength, and ever-present help in trouble." But God seemed so far away.

By the time the doctor in Traverse City discharged me from the hospital, my hands had dug deeply into the bed rails. I asked once more before we left, "Please take me home? I want to go home."

My eyes were red and puffy and my throat ached from endless crying, but Ted took the steering wheel and faced due north to the family cabin. The loss of another baby and the heartfelt desire to go home shattered any hopes for healing in our marriage. Ted refused to be the person of the hour, the husband I needed so desperately.

That week, I walked in circles around the cabin and on the trails. The fresh pine and the shade of the trees were protection from the sun and the rain. The tears were buried deep inside, and to avoid my in-laws, I stayed outside and rested in the warm sunshine during the day. I walked to the end of a long, narrow driveway thinking I could escape the cabin and find a way home. Why didn't I pick up the keys and just take our car?

Something deep inside kept me from even thinking of doing such a thing. Once again, the words under my breath were, "I hate you."

When Ted finally took me home, my emotions were raw. I cried at the drop of a hat. Lost and alone with my grief and sorrow, I isolated. I shared with no one the deep hurt inside. I grieved as I touched and smelled the tiny clothes that were lying in the baby's room, and I grieved because of my failure to deliver a healthy baby. Inadequacy as a wife ruled my life, and now for the second time, I came home with empty arms and an empty heart.

Isolation lasted for a little more than six weeks. I know now that isolation and denial lengthen the pain, but back then, it seemed the only thing to do. Focusing on my own circumstances led me farther from God and farther from others. Friends tried to redirect me, but stubbornness in my heart did not allow them into my life.

Cast Your Cares

Cast your cares on The Lord
and he will sustain you; he
will never let the righteous fall.
—Psalm 55:22

My friend Sue came over unannounced one morning about three weeks later. She was a stubborn perky woman who was not afraid to knock and let herself in. "Get cleaned up and be ready to go for lunch in thirty minutes. I will be waiting in the car."

"Absolutely not. I am staying home."

"Absolutely not was not in the equation. You are going."

She left me no excuse. I cleaned up as quickly as possible, and we were off to a quiet little restaurant on the other side of town. When we entered the restaurant, the first thing I saw were the golden-brown muffins. They looked and smelled heavenly. My nose tingled, and my taste buds watered. I had not eaten much in days. She ordered for both of us, not listening to my objections. When the quiche and muffins arrived, she prayed and we began to eat. She started to talk about the challenges I was facing. "You know how good God is, don't you?" She fixed her eyes on mine waiting for a response.

"I don't know how good God is."

"You are here with me, eating and talking. You have two eyes, two hands, two feet, and so much more." Sue's eyes began to tear as she held out her hands to take mine. "Cast all your cares upon Him, Lindsey. He cares about you."

She didn't stop to take a breath. She talked about finding something worthwhile to do. "Maybe you should get a job or start volunteering at church. It might boost your self-esteem. You know you are loved and needed."

I had not given a thought to anything but my own grief. Her words were so true. I had not cast any of my cares on God but rather tried hanging on to them in my closed heart. I did not say a word until we got to the car. Then the tears started falling and the words on their heels. "I am sorry. My heart feels so empty."

"I haven't a clue as to what you are going through, but God does." My heart aches for you, but you can make a choice whether you are going to stay where you are or move forward. Cast your cares upon Him."

When she dropped me off, my life was the same, but somehow my perspective had changed. I started volunteering at church, and I went job hunting. At church, I began to work with the teen girls, something I had done when I was first married. The job I found wasn't a dream job, but it took my mind off failure and on success. I actually had fun running the huge printing presses and seeing how many pages I could collate in one hour.

Ted's career still kept him away from home and close to his parents. I was often lonely but no longer so desperate. Revelation 21:4a reads, "God will wipe every tear from their eyes."

God was wiping away my tears. With my second paycheck I purchased a brilliant opal ring with two small diamonds. The opal represented my life and the two small diamonds, the lives of my two stillborn children.

My world remained constant for one year. We both continued working, and while he played golf, I was outside walking or inside quilting and cross-stitching. Consistency felt good, and I lulled myself into believing it would remain.

As consistency lulled me, the inevitable shocked me. The queasy feeling that accompanies pregnancy once again woke me early one morning. Fear gripped me as the memories of the past invaded my thoughts. "God, I cannot be pregnant. I cannot endure the loss of another baby."

Dr. Post was not as reassuring this time. He wanted my life to be as stress free as possible, to stay off my feet, and he said, "Eat."

Stress, as stress free as possible. Did he have any idea what my life was like? Did he know about the verbal and emotional abuse that took place on a regular basis? No, he did not because I had not told him. My thinking: hidden secrets are best-kept secrets.

Although I tried to eat, nothing stayed down. It was a vicious cycle of eating and being sick or not eating and being sick. One stressor compiled upon another. The final stressor came when I was approximately four months pregnant.

Ted came home after one of his business trips with news he could not wait to share. "I want to be a pastor. I am going to seminary."

"You are what? Why now?" I had no idea what to think about this drastic change.

"Listen," he exclaimed. "I know that God is calling me."

"How can you be so sure? What will your parents say?" I couldn't help but think of their reaction to this news. It would not be one of joy. In fact, they would most likely be angry.

There was no rationale, no thought-out, prayed-out explanation for this quick decision. He had made up his mind. The blessing for me was that he would be *forced* to leave his parents' side. There was no way he could work for them and go to school.

My thoughts turned to survival. "How are we going to keep a home and have food on the table without an income?" We had finally settled in a home for more than one year, and I liked the feeling. My mind raced as I struggled with thoughts of the child I was carrying and the uncertainty of the future.

I watched as he told his family, as he registered for seminary, and as he looked for a less expensive place to live. I continued to stay off my feet, but my stress level was at an all-time high. "God, are you really calling him into full-time ministry? If you are, then why don't I feel the same calling?"

I was seven months pregnant when my family helped Ted move our belongings into a different place. He was already taking classes, and his parents had cleverly convinced him that working part-time in the family business would be much wiser than looking for a job elsewhere. To meet budget needs, my car was sold. His rationale: "You cannot drive while you are pregnant."

Without a car, I depended on Ted to take me to my doctor appointments. His promise was always the same, "I will be there on time." Because I wanted to believe him so badly, I didn't have a backup plan. When I missed an appointment, it was Dr. Post who called, not his receptionist. He reprimanded me very sternly.

"You have less than one month to go. It is crucial that I see you at each appointment."

He didn't have to tell me. I knew how important my appointments were, and he knew how important it was for me to rest and stay calm. What he didn't know was the true reason I didn't make my appointment and the stress that permeated my life. I cried as I promised, "I won't miss again."

As I hung up the phone, I made a very important decision. "Sue, will you be a backup driver if I need someone to take me to see Dr. Post? Ted travels so much, and I need to make sure I don't miss any appointments.

"Did you miss one of your scheduled appointments?"

"Yes, it couldn't be helped. Ted was gone, and I forgot the appointment."

"No, you didn't. Ted didn't come home to take you. Why don't you stop denying what is happening in your home? Your best friends seem to know."

"What are you talking about? Nothing is happening in our home. Please do not discuss missing appointments with anyone. Gossip travels far too quickly."

"I won't, and I will pick you up. But it would be nice if you would confide in someone."

"I have nothing to talk about. Thank you for your concern."

Dr. Post allowed me to go one week past my due date and then concern over past pregnancies prompted him to induce labor. On one hand, I was elated, and on the other full of fear over what if. "Just because I have come this far doesn't necessarily mean I will come home with a baby in my arms."

As Ted drove me to the hospital that morning, he commented, "Friends at the seminary are praying. You may think it is impossible, but it is not." In Luke 18:27, Jesus said, "What is impossible with men is possible with God." Very seldom was he encouraging, and I accepted it gratefully.

Dr. Post greeted us at the hospital and assured us that every precaution was being taken for the delivery of a healthy baby. The room I entered looked much the same as the room I entered when both of the other babies were born. The myriad of machines, the IV setup, and the heart monitor for both myself and the baby caused little concern. The challenges of past pregnancies gave me little hope of an easy delivery. The nurse immediately wrapped me in blankets, and Dr. Post examined me one more time. Finally, he broke my water. The IV had already been inserted, and not long after, Pitocin begin to slowly enter my bloodstream. Surprisingly, it didn't take long for labor to begin. Labor pains were not hard, and at some point during the next two hours, my doctor's assistant came in and said, "This could take a long time. Hang in there."

When he came back forty-five minutes later, he placed his hand on my stomach and said, "Stop pushing."

"I am not pushing," I replied.

"Yes, you are pushing. You may not realize it, but it is too early to push." He examined me and quickly called for Dr. Post to meet us in the delivery room.

"Try not to push until we get into the delivery room. Your baby is ready to come into this world."

I was still gritting my teeth and whispering, "I am not pushing." The nurses didn't hear me. They were rushing me down the hall and into the delivery room. Dr. Post was still putting on his gloves when that precious little bundle began to pop his head out.

His sigh of relief and his words of affirmation were ones I had waited to hear for so long. He announced to the world, "You have a healthy baby boy." I cried as he handed me our son. This brand new baby boy was a miracle, a blessing from God.

I had read Psalm 127:3 early that morning: "Don't you see that children are God's best gift? The fruit of the womb his generous legacy?" I had two children in heaven and now was holding a precious son, a gift from God. We had already decided that if our baby was a boy, we would name him Joshua David. Joshua trusted God when the Israelites were told to spy out the Promised Land, and at one point, God called Joshua a man after His own heart.

At the moment I prayed, "God, let him be called a man after your heart and give him what he needs to trust you all the days of his life."

As I held him, tears of joy fell down my cheeks. He was so tiny and soft. Everything about him was perfect, including his tiny head with little tufts of golden blonde hair, his perfect fingers and toes, and his soft squeal of delight. It was difficult to give him to his father and even more difficult to see him go to the nursery.

"If I give him up, you might not bring him back."

"I will bring him back after you have had some rest, and you may not know this, but you are free to walk down to the nursery whenever you would like.

"I will be down right away." That is what I envisioned as I sighed and dozed off into a peaceful sleep. I dreamed of Joshua David wrapped in a blue blanket with his head peeking out. When I woke up, I had just enough time to sit up and wash my face and hands. I could feel the excitement as I heard the nurse coming down the hallway. *How much longer?* I pondered. And then he was back, cleaned up, crying, and ready to eat.

The joy I felt as I once again held Joshua David was beyond words. He was seven pounds and four ounces. He was just as I remembered him when I first took him in my arms, except he was clean. I held him closely as I said, "I love you so much. You are a special gift from God, Joshua David."

Due to the stress of the pregnancy, I was advised to bottle-feed the baby. Reality began to sink in as I tried to get him to take the nipple. "You sure do have a lot to learn," I said to myself as I watched him do what would soon become natural. "It takes time," the nurses reassured me.

"I have all the time in the world."

Two days later, we came home. Ted dropped us off and then left to play a round of golf. "I need the break before I get back into work and studying." I bit my tongue as the words formed in my mouth. Thank goodness I didn't say what I was thinking. I intended to enjoy the moment even if he wasn't there.

Challenges

Joshua David was a delightful baby, born at a time when Ted's schooling was in full swing. Ted's pattern of being late followed him into seminary and into completing school papers. Caring for Joshua, keeping the house clean, and typing his papers left me exhausted.

His papers caused us the most contention. I could not decipher his writing, and when it came to words in Greek, well let's just say, "It was all Greek to me."

I pleaded, "Please have them done two days before they are due, or I will not type them. Can't you help me that much?" They were never done, and I always gave in, many times staying up all night to complete them. When I thought the papers were typed perfectly, Ted would proofread them once more for any additional errors.

"The Greek words are spelled wrong."

"I can't read your English, let alone your Greek. I could look up the words if they were more legible and if you had the papers done earlier."

Frustration mounted as I returned to the typewriter to fix the errors. As I typed, Josh would laugh and play. His smile displayed contentment, and his naturally spiked golden tufts of hair were a constant reminder of his effervescent personality. "Thank you, God, for the miracle of life. Remind me often of your provision."

Joshua loved to play both day and night. His agenda did not include sleep. Everyone I asked had a different solution. My mom said, "Don't let him take a long nap."

"Mom, I've tried that. Short naps, long naps, early and late naps."

Sue said, "Drive around until he falls asleep."

I drove him around, and Josh would finally fall asleep. But when I turned in the driveway, he would wake up as if he knew we were home.

Ted said, "You are spoiling him."

"If you think I am spoiling him, then you stay up with him and see if you can function during the day."

"He just wants to play. He could be screaming."

I had exhausted myself and had learned one thing. Their suggestions didn't work. He wanted to play until three or four in the morning, and the dark circles under my eyes were evidence of what I wanted and needed so desperately. I was supplementing our meager income by babysitting, and I had no choice but to get up before the children began coming at seven.

"Can't we take turns watching him at night?"

"I have to go to school tomorrow. I can't stay up."

"Even one night a week would help."

One night a week was too much to ask. I continued to try as much as possible to keep up with everything. Even when Josh did sleep, I always had papers to finish. In the midst of this turmoil came news from Dr. Post.

"You are pregnant again. What were you thinking?"

"I didn't think I could get pregnant this soon." I wouldn't tell him how slim the opportunities were for me to even be pregnant. The despair was written all over my face.

Dr. Post replied, "I am sorry. I should not have responded so negatively. You are going to have another healthy baby."

I wasn't so sure, but with Joshua cradled in my arms and proof of pregnancy in my purse, I meandered home. I was in no hurry, although in my heart I knew Ted would be gone. The house was empty when I arrived. I had time to get supper in the oven and try to focus on Josh and the paper that was due the next day.

Ted arrived in time for a late dinner, one that had to be reheated. Would that ever change? How many times would he eat alone before he made the choice to be home in close proximity to the time he predicted?

I had already eaten and was ready to tell him the news of my pregnancy, but before I could say anything, he was telling me about his golf game.

"I shot three under par at Sunnybrook Country Club. That's not great, but it is good enough to put me in the lineup for this weekend's tournament."

"Could you please stop for a moment? I have something I want to tell you."

"Can't it wait until later? I have some paperwork to do and a test to study for."

"No, it can't wait. I am pregnant."

"What! You are pregnant. What were you thinking?"

"No, what were *you* thinking?" Why does this pregnancy seem to be all my fault? It takes two to make a baby, you know."

"Why right now? I am in school, we already have Josh and well, the timing is way off. How will you take care of two?"

Taking care of two wasn't really the issue at this point. The reality of pregnancy was sickness and exhaustion. How would I babysit for other families, take care of Joshua, and stay off my feet during this pregnancy? Help with our income was no longer an option. I would not be able to take care of other children when I was already beginning to feel the side effects of being pregnant.

One by one, I called the parents. "Yes, I am pregnant. No, you don't understand. I have to be off my feet. I don't know how I will take care of Josh. Thank you."

Finally, I was finished. Tears trickled down my cheeks.

"Yes, God, I want another child more than anything else. But how will I carry another child to term?"

I heard that still small voice, "Trust me. I promised that I will be with you always."

"It's too soon. I can't keep up with Ted's papers now. How will I if this pregnancy is like the others?"

"Focus on today. Let me take care of the rest."

Back and forth, I talked to God. Fortunately, that night Josh did fall asleep and I had time to rest and reflect on God's goodness and love. He had been with me through each of my pregnancies, and He would be with me now.

Ted consumed himself with school, work, and golf. I had to quit serving at church, but not one person asked why. I followed Dr. Post's orders to the best of my ability. I was doing everything right when everything went wrong. I saw the telltale sign of problems early one evening.

"It will stop," I said to myself. "I can't lose another baby. I can't!"

But it did not stop. Even though I stayed off my feet for the following two days, it did not stop. I sat stoically as Ted drove to the hospital, and I sobbed uncontrollably as Dr. Post informed me that the baby inside me was no longer living.

That afternoon, Dr. Post performed a dilation and curettage (D&C) and then he left me alone to rest. When he finally returned to the room, he hugged me and then stated rather firmly. "No more pregnancies for two years. You must give your body a rest. I almost lost you when you gave birth to your first child. I don't want that to happen and neither do you. Eat, enjoy your time with Josh, and check in with me in two weeks."

Exactly two weeks later, I heard Dr. Post repeat his instructions. "No pregnancy for two years."

"Don't worry. There are no babies on the horizon. I promise."

A Rocky Road

The following two years were rocky, to say the least. Juggling Ted's schooling, our church ministry, and taking care of Josh weren't easy. Often, we were out until one to one thirty in the morning. Bible studies didn't go that late, but the meeting after the study did. It never seemed to bother Ted, but I was ready to go home when the study ended. When we finally got in the car, the confrontation would begin.

"Why can't we go home at a reasonable time?"

"I wanted to talk to the guys about school."

"But Josh doesn't sleep, and at least I have a chance to get him in bed if we are home."

"What we were talking about was important. Why don't you talk to the women?"

"I don't know what to say to them. When the Bible study is over, I am ready to go home and try to get some sleep."

I didn't want to talk to the women. I allowed no one into my life. There was always that closed door on what happened in our home. Ted was very seldom present. Even if he was in the room, it was as if he was not there. His berating hadn't stopped, and now his parents had one more thing to talk about. I was not an overprotective mother and that was their expectation.

I heard my mother's voice, "You are called to forgive, but not to forget." She was so right. The old saying "Sticks and stones will break my bones, but words will never hurt me" was certainly not true. The degrading words of my husband and his parents pierced to the very bottom of my soul.

I was filled with fear when I found out that I was pregnant again. We hadn't waited long enough, but I had miscalculated, and the one time was the right time. When I told Ted, he didn't seem all that concerned.

"They will grow up together,"

"But Dr. Post said two years."

"It's almost two years."

"I don't want to lose another child. It's too soon. Dr. Post said two years."

Although the thought of losing another child was heavy on my heart, the joy of having Josh was a reminder of how wonderful it would be to have another.

Dr. Post was quick to remind me to stay home and rest. This was a blessing in disguise that I had no way of anticipating. I no longer had to stay out until all hours of the night. I could rest while Josh played. I was sick; but Josh, as little as he was, would come running to me. "Mommy, mommy, okay?"

Serenity was born on the first day of spring, a delivery that was relatively easy as compared to the others. She was contented, and she actually slept. She was beautiful in every way. Her dark curly hair, big brown eyes, and tanned skin caused people to stop and stare. She smiled and cooed, seeming to be as contented as her brother when he was born. The first few weeks were any mother's dream. Then came a huge change. She started screaming constantly. There was nothing I could do to stop her.

Suggestions were made. Change formula, change bottles, hold her differently, get her to burp, and the list went on. Finally, her pediatrician said, "She has colic."

"What is colic?"

"It is severe, often fluctuating pain caused by gas build up in the stomach."

"What can I do? She seems to be in constant pain."

"I can offer suggestions and give her medicine, but it may or may not help. Please don't think it's something you are doing."

That thought had entered my mind. Wasn't everything I did wrong? I used different bottles, gave her different formula, and held her every imaginable way in hopes that something would help. My mother came at least once a week to give me a much-needed timeout.

I was still trying to keep up with Ted's papers, care for Josh and Serenity, and serve at our local church when finances dictated that we move again. This was our fifth move, and chaos became a normal part of our day. As we searched for less expensive housing, packed our belongings, and moved into yet another home, Ted's parents became concerned.

He was their baby, the youngest child, and they did not like the fact that he was under financial stress. Right then, I had no inkling of their concern, nor did I care. I already was carrying more than I could handle, and my stress level was once again at an all-time high.

Priorities had to be made, and ministry seemed to be the only way to relieve the stress that was beginning to consume me.

"You have to be home with the children."

"I can still serve as assistant youth group leader if you help with the children."

"I have work and school, and that comes first."

"This ministry is so important to me. I'm typing your papers and helping as much as possible. If you didn't play golf as much and were here for us just a little, I could still serve."

"No, my decision holds."

I was devastated and guilt ridden. The ministry that I loved was being stripped from me, and I was letting God and the youth group down. The teens did not see it that way. They rallied around me in love. They volunteered to play with Josh while I focused on Serenity. If I had continued ministering to them, they would have missed the opportunity of ministering to me.

It was six months before Serenity was finally free of colic. In those six months, I learned what Philippians 4:13 meant. "I can do all things through Christ who strengthens me." Knowing Serenity was in pain and there was nothing we could do often brought me to my knees. It was only God's strength that enabled me to persevere.

As He carried me through this season, I was challenged with another. Ted's parents had continued to fume over our financial condition. I learned the hard way that over the past months, this had been a topic of discussion, a discussion that I had no part in.

It had been a long time since both children were in bed and sleeping at a reasonable hour. The ring of the doorbell caused me to jump. Ted seemed to know someone was coming and quickly opened the door to welcome his family into our home. We sat around the living room. I hesitated, but they quickly encouraged me to sit down. I had no idea what to expect, but it was obvious they were not there to see the children or visit. A one-way conversation began, and Ted and I were expected to listen.

"You are the one who made him go to school to become a minister."

"You are killing your mother with this nonsense."

"Why can't you just continue in the family business?"

Their anger boiled and spilled out in our home that night. I listened in disbelief as they spewed out words of disgust and hatred, much of it directed at me. When they finally stopped talking, Ted opened the door and invited them to leave. I was trembling as they exited our home. My eyes were brimming with tears as I stepped out of the living room and into the bedroom. My thinking—they could stay away forever.

Gratitude

As the long, cold days of winter turned to spring, the new life within me changed as well. I held my hands to my stomach, delighted to feel the baby wiggle and kick. I continually prayed for the tiny life inside me.

"This baby will be strong and healthy," I told Kelly and Stacy.

"How long do you think it will be?" Stacy asked.

"The baby is due the first of July. Not too much longer."

Stacy and Kelly were as excited as our family. They wanted it to be soon. So did I. I was finishing the last of Ted's papers, taking care of the children, and preparing for the birth of this baby.

Ted had been looking and watching for churches that were without pastors. When he was called to visit a church, they wanted to see the family.

"I know how important this is, but it is becoming more and more difficult for me to get the children ready and be out for a day."

"Yes, but I can't go unless you are there. They want to meet you, and you know how important this is to me."

"I understand, but what about the baby? Six weeks is not much time, and I have gone with you on every other visit."

"Last one, I promise. And this could be the church we are called to. It's only a few hours from home, and you can probably rest in the middle of the day."

His words took me a little by surprise. I had not felt the same calling as Ted. I had prayed for the calling to be a pastor's wife during his years at Grand Rapids Baptist College and Seminary, but I never felt the impelling call to become one. My only desire was to be submissive to my husband. I reflected for just a moment on his seminary years. The pregnancies that were not successful, the turmoil between Ted and myself, and the night when his family had arrived to berate me even more. No, I did not feel the calling, but I would go because that is what I had to do.

I packed the children's things the night before. Although I was awake most of the night, the children slept peacefully. I checked on them often, realizing that the following day would be difficult for them as well. They were imperfect children, with the expectation to be perfect for one day.

The day of our visit brought both children into our bedroom very early in the morning. "We are ready to go," they screamed. "We ate cereal and are done. All done."

Cereal was dripping from head to toe, and Josh had already dressed himself. "Well, little man, I guess a change of clothes is in order. Hurry to the bathroom, and I will clean you up."

"I was hungry and gave some to Serenity, too."

"You are a big boy and you talk so well. But now we have to hurry and get cleaned up. It's time to go."

We arrived with no time to spare and entered the church as one happy family. What happened in our home I hid so well. Ted preached; I modeled the perfect wife, and the children were very well behaved. The church seemed to receive Ted's message, and the congregation was excited about the new addition to our family. The day was long, but I persevered.

On the way home, Ted said as much to himself as to me, "I believe that is going to be our first church."

As I was dozing off, I wondered if he was right. If God called him to this church, there were so many things we would have to do. But right now, I had to turn my mind off and get some sleep.

I woke up in the middle of the night with a quiet peace. "I am in labor, I think. I'm not certain, but I think so."

"Are you sure?" Ted asked. "Maybe this is false labor."

"Possibly, but I don't think so. Let me lay quiet and see if the pain goes away." It did stop, but two days later began again. This time, I was certain it was the real thing. Five weeks before my due date, I was in the car and on my way to the hospital. Dr. Post was there to greet us as he had always been, and his reassurance gave me hope. "The baby seems big enough, and the heartbeat is strong. We won't know about the lungs until after the birth."

Six hours later, Jonilynn burst into the world. She weighed just a little under five pounds, with lungs fully developed and a cry that reached the other end of the neonatal unit. I had chosen to name her after Joni Erickson-Tada, a woman of strength and courage. Somehow, I knew that she would need extra strength as she grew to be a woman of God.

Joshua and Serenity stayed with my parents for one week while I stayed in the hospital with Jonilynn. After one week of separation from the other children, with a new baby in my arms, we drove straight to my parents. They were anxious to see Jonilynn again and to have a chance to hold her. Josh and Serenity were ready to see her as well, and after hugging me, they checked out their new sister. Josh was especially curious. "Hi, baby sister," were the first words out of his mouth.

He lost interest quickly when he saw Grandpa leading the team of horses out of the barn. "Can we go with Grandpa and Grandma one more time with the horses and the wagon?"

Mom and Dad would not have cared, but I wanted the children to come home. It had been a long week, and I knew we would have to come back to get them later if they stayed. Thankfulness over-flowed from my heart as I reached out and hugged mom. "Thank you for all you've done. We appreciate it."

As we turned at the corner to our street, we heard the sirens out in the country. We gave it no thought as we turned into our driveway and started to unpack the car. The children began to play as their baby sister slept in the car. The phone rang, and I ran to get it, expecting it to be friends from church. Instead, my oldest brother Dennis spoke in a very quiet voice. "Dad and Mom have been in an accident with the horses and wagon. We don't know how badly, but they are on the way to the trauma center in Grand Rapids. I will let you know as soon as I know something. For now, stay put with that new baby.

We waited anxiously for the next call to come. While we were waiting, my thoughts turned to our children. 'What if they had not come home with us? What if they had been on the wagon with their grandpa and grandma?'

When the call finally came, my brother's voice reflected urgency. I knew the situation couldn't be good.

"You should get someone to watch the children. Mom is now in critical condition. Dad will not leave mother's side even though he should be in a room of his own. The horses spooked, and when mom flew off the wagon, she hit the left side of her forehead on a telephone pole. Her brain is beginning to swell, so they are drilling a small hole this evening to allow the pressure on the brain to be relieved. They are not sure she is going to make it. Come as soon as you can."

There was a couple in the church who loved our children and treated them as their own. They often offered to babysit, and after the phone call from my brother, their names were the first to come to mind.

"My mom is in the trauma center at Butterworth Hospital in Grand Rapids. Can you watch the children?" I pleaded.

"Do you want us to stay there? The kids may be more content, and you can leave as soon as we get there."

They arrived in less than fifteen minutes. We had no idea how many times throughout the next two months they would be watching our children. When the calls came that my mother might not make it through the night, they appeared as if by magic. The children were delighted to see our friends, making the burden of leaving them so much lighter.

"How can I thank you?" I asked each time they came.

"We are being thanked each time we watch the kids. I long to have children, and taking care of yours fills the void if only for a season."

We arrived at the hospital the first night in time to see my mom before she slipped into a coma. We joined together in prayer. It was a minute-by-minute, hour-by-hour situation. We talked to her, gently caressed her, and read the Bible to her, not knowing if she could hear us but knowing that this is what the doctors told us to do. Dad recovered slowly, as his injuries were not as extreme. The road rash and bruises did not keep him from being at Mom's bedside as much as possible.

There came a time when we had no choice but to begin taking turns staying with her, and finally, we had to leave her alone some of the time. Dad had to work, and Ted had papers and school to finish. My two brothers and sister had to get on with their lives as well. We were visiting Mom often but no longer staying with her at the hospital.

Late in August, early on a Sunday morning, Dennis went to visit Mom. He told us later, "I talked to her doctor and then walked into her room. When I said 'hi' to her, she opened her eyes and said 'hi' to me. I almost fainted."

We rallied around her late that morning as she slipped in and out of the comma. It was the beginning of a long and arduous journey. We watched her take baby steps to recovery. God was with her each step of the way, and when Thanksgiving came, we had dinner as a family at my parent's house. I cooked turkey, and everyone shared in preparing the rest of the meal. The food wasn't nearly as important as the miracle of having her home. It was more than we could ever have imagined. The prayer offered that Thanksgiving was one of deep gratitude for all God had done.

Attacked Again

The summer of the accident was also when Ted accepted the call to our first pastorate. I answered the phone and quickly turned it over to him.

"Yes, you have the right number. I am Ted."

"The church board has voted, and we want you to be the next pastor of our church."

"It will be my first pastorate. Are you certain?"

"Yes, we are certain. Talk it over with your wife and get back to me."

"When would you like us to be there?"

"Before school starts. Fall is a new beginning for so many things. Earlier would be nicer, but we understand with a family how difficult it must be to pick up and move."

"I will talk to Lindsey, but I know we want to accept the call."

"Call me back after you have had the weekend to pray. Let me know then."

I overheard the conversation and knew full well that he would accept.

Moving to a new community, the fulfillment of Ted's dream, and a move away from his parents were thoughts that would now become reality. It was an extremely busy time. My mom's accident, combined with a new baby, and graduation made it difficult, but this would be our first church. I listened to music and danced to the beat as I began to pack. Ted traveled to meet his church board and to find a home to rent. He came home satisfied with the trip.

"They would have loved to get to know you a little better, but I explained the circumstances of your mom's accident. They understood. And I found an older two-story home to rent right in the downtown area. I know you will like it."

"I would like to see it before we rent it. I will be living there too."

"I had to take it. You will like it, I promise."

I had heard those promise words from Ted on many different occasions and didn't have a good reason to trust them, but I had no choice. Ted had already signed the lease. I would have to trust God for the outcome.

The summer passed in a blur. I felt as if I saw myself coming in the door at the same time I was leaving. There were papers to finish, diapers to change, toilet training that needed to happen, packing that needed to be done, and a mom that needed to be visited.

When it was time to start moving boxes to our new house, I decided it was best to leave the children home.

"I agree, but you do realize that I can't watch them. I have two more papers to complete."

"I will figure it out. You get your papers done so I can type them."

"I'll get them done early."

My plan fell into place quickly. I would ask the neighbors across the street to babysit while I was gone. It seemed a perfect plan. Their oldest son Don agreed to go with me to bring boxes into the house. He would even help pack and load the boxes.

The sun peeking in the window on the morning of our first day of moving gave clear indication that it would be a grand day. The children would have fun with the neighbors and I would be able to pack and unpack boxes with no thought of rain. The children's things were in their bags, and they were dressed and fed before nine. I walked them across the street and returned with their son to begin packing the already full boxes. We moved quickly and were soon in the truck driving to the new house.

"Do you have any idea what the house looks like?"

"I haven't seen it. You and I will be the first, and I am just a little nervous."

"Wow. You are moving into a house you have not seen. That's pretty brave."

"I do not have much choice. Ted signed the lease before I could see it. He insisted that the owners couldn't wait."

"Hopefully it will be something you like. My mom would never move sight unseen."

"Sometimes you have to do what you have to do, Don. It will be an adventure."

With our constant chatter, the two-hour drive passed quickly. I saw the huge oak tree Ted had told me about as we rounded the last corner. It marked the entrance to our driveway. It also was home to a wonderful swing. I knew immediately the children would love it. I parked the truck and walked back to the tree to be the first to swing in the tree swing. My legs dangled freely as I anticipated opening the door to our new home.

I returned to the truck to grab the key and anxiously walked to the front door. What would my home be like? Would it be remotely clean? Some of the homes I had moved into were nasty. Would it have any light-colored paint on the walls? Dark paint tended to bring me down. I cautiously turned the key and opened the door.

What I saw pleased me. It was dingy, but it was clean. I opened cupboards and closets. Everything was clean. Even the oven and refrigerator were clean. The dingy walls filled almost every room, but I knew what to do about that. A little inexpensive paint and a little swear equity would take care of that.

Don and I unpacked the truck then decided to grab something to eat and head for home. I had more boxes to pack and papers to type. We could come another day. I left feeling satisfied with a positive day under my belt.

When we arrived home, Don quickly helped me clean out the truck.

"See you when you come to pick up the kids. I had better go home. I am sure Mom will be happy to see me."

"I will be over shortly. I can't wait to see the children. But first I am going to check on my mom."

Ted met me at the door. He appeared anxious. I knew immediately something had gone wrong. Without a cell phone, I had no idea if my mom had taken a turn for the worse or if something was wrong with the children. I did not have to wait.

"The neighbors took the kids for a walk, and when they walked by my parent's house, my mother grabbed the stroller and Serenity. She will not let her come home until you go to get her."

"What? You did not go get her."

"Our neighbor made it very clear. Unless you get her, my parents will not let her come home."

"Yes, I know that, but you didn't even try to get her?"

"No. They said you had to come."

I put on tennis shoes and walked the half block to the children's grandparents. They met me in the garage, with Serenity wrapped tightly in a blanket. I did not have a chance to open my mouth.

"You are not fit to be a mother, let alone the mother of our grandchildren. How can you say you are a good mother when you leave the children with the neighbor's?"

I listened to their berating until I saw an opportunity to grab Serenity out of their arms. I did not reach for the stroller. There was no need. I ran all the way home, trying to stay composed. Serenity was already frantic. She did not need to see me out of control. I laid her gently in her crib and began to rub her back, trying to calm her tender body. She was shaking, and I so desperately wanted to cry. The tears rolled down my cheeks, but still I did not cry out. There would be time enough for that later. I picked her up and walked to the door to greet the other children.

Joshua was anxious to tell me what had happened. "Grandpa and Grandma took Serenity. They would not let her come with us."

"I know. Daddy told me. But she is safe now. Why don't you sing for me?"

As he began to sing, the children and I joined in. When every-one was settled and I could escape, I ran to my bedroom and began to sob.

How could they be so cruel? What had I done that I deserved such treatment?

I cried until all tears were gone then washed my face and went around the house locking the doors. Locks would keep everyone out and my family safe. I did not understand that locks keep no one out when one's heart is bleeding so badly. I needed to open up to some-one, but there was no one. I did not dare share with anyone.

New Beginnings

After my first trip to our new home and the incident that followed, the children were attached to my hip. Their grandparents made no effort to reconcile, and I wanted the door locked each time I put something into the car or truck. Fear controlled my life. Would they try to take one of the other children? The thought of Hastings, Michigan, enticed me more and more.

Driven to be ready, I kept moving at a frantic pace, a pace that enabled us to have the truck packed and the apartment cleaned early on moving day. I had the children in the car and the seatbelts hooked when I saw Ted's parents coming down the street. I looked at Ted. "I'm getting in the car with the children and leaving now."

"Don't you want to say goodbye?"

"No. I want to leave before anything else happens. Just tell them goodbye for me."

As I was about to lock the car door, I recalled the words of my mother. "God doesn't ask you to trust or forget, but He does ask that you forgive."

"And how am I going to forgive them?"

My mind raced as they walked up the driveway. Every part of my being wanted to run, but God reminded me of His love and protection. I unbuckled the car seats, unlocked the doors, and helped Josh and Serenity out of their seats. I picked Jonilynn up from her seat and held her tightly as we approached their grandparents. Serenity was trembling, and her eyes filled with tears.

"We wanted to walk over and say goodbye."

I was at a total loss for words. I couldn't say I would miss them or that I was sorry to go. The only words that came to mind were, "Goodbye. I will take good care of your grandchildren." I helped the children get back into their seats, and as I got into the car, I turned and said, "Maybe you can visit us sometime?" Where that came from, I don't know. But it opened the door for the healing of a very fractured relationship between two families.

His parents said, "Thank you," and waited for Ted to leave with the truck. I only imagined what they said after we left. Did it matter? We would be over two hours apart, and fear would no longer reign in our home. In a very short time, we would officially be a pastor's family.

Ted reminded me, "Take your time. We have plenty of daylight left, and I won't be far behind."

I turned a pale shade of green as I pulled out of the driveway. My stomach turned inside out. Why had I said they could visit sometime? What was I thinking? Could it be that I was already beginning to have an attitude of forgiveness?

Jill Bolte Taylor said, "To experience peace does not mean that your life is always blissful. It means that you are capable of tapping into a blissful state of mind amidst the normal chaos of a hectic life."

Leaving in a state of confusion and bewilderment caused wrong turns and many pit stops. Serenity continued to be teary-eyed. From the mouth of a babe came words that tugged at my heart. "I don't think Grandpa and Grandma love me. Grandma scared me."

Josh responded, "Don't cry. We are going to live a long way away, and they won't come and visit us."

"Josh, let's sing. Maybe Serenity will sing with us?" Joni is sleeping, and we can sing quietly.

Immediately, Josh, my talker, began to sing his rendition of "This Little Light of Mine."

"That's what we need to do, Serenity. Shine our light so Grandpa and Grandma know about Jesus. Mommy, you know. Sing with me."

Conviction was heavy on my heart, and singing the words humbled me as I thought about how Jesus treated people who had been so hurtful. "God, please help me to love them somehow or at least forgive them."

"Come on, Mommy. Sing, don't talk."

And as I sang, I tapped into a blissful state of mind amidst the normal chaos of a hectic life. I missed two turns while singing with Josh but realized quickly I needed to turn around.

I wonder how many times God gently reminds me of choices and I choose my way instead of following Him?

My thoughts were interrupted when Serenity asked, "Are we almost there?"

"Yes, sweetie, we are almost there. Let's stop at the next gas station for a pop ice."

"Yay, can we, please? I'm thirsty."

"Me too. Josh and Joni are probably thirsty too. And while we are there, you both need to use the bathroom."

Josh piped up, "What about Jonilynn? She slept all the way. Does she get something too?"

"Yes, she gets changed diapers and a bottle. Maybe some Cheerios? Today has been a long day, and it's only two o'clock. We'll be there soon."

Everyone was ready for the last part of our adventure, and after passing the maple tree that would have taken at least six people to embrace, we were home. Josh immediately saw the tree swing. The twinkle in his eyes told me exactly what he was thinking.

"Give Mommy time to find the toilet paper and the towels from the car. We'll use the bathroom and put Joni in her stroller."

"Hurry, Mommy, let's go." I followed his directions and we were at the tree in no time.

I forgot all about the time and about the chaos that was waiting for me at home. The delight of watching the children play in the swing refreshed and exhilarated my entire being. It didn't take long, and I had Joni in the swing with me. As little as she was, she squealed and laughed as much as the others.

When we finally left, over an hour had lapsed. I fully expected the truck to be parked in the driveway when we arrived. The driveway was empty, and there were no visible signs that he had arrived. I had no way of calling him, so I put Josh and Serenity in an empty corner of the living room with Legos while Joni sat in the stroller and watched me unpack the car.

I was just about finished when Ted came around the corner. My dad followed close behind. I had no idea he was coming.

"I thought you might be able to use a little help. Your cousin Ruth is staying with your mother, and I decided on the spur of the moment to spend some time helping you unload the truck. Is that okay with you?"

Wow. I had no idea you were coming. "Of course, it's okay. And thank you. I'm looking at a truckload of furniture and things, and the truck has to be back in the morning."

"Well, let's get started."

"What about the children? They will never put up with this commotion."

"I've got that all taken care of." Just then, out popped my brother Jim from behind the truck door. "Look who I brought to help with the children." Jim grinned from ear to ear as he scrambled into the house to look for his nieces and nephews.

"Thank you again. There is no way this could have been finished by tomorrow without your help. What a surprise."

The children were able to sleep in their beds that night. After moving ten times, I knew how to pack and mark well.

Everything that is, but bathroom towels. "Mommy, we don't have any big towels. I can't take a shower."

"We can shower tomorrow. I have looked everywhere and can't find the towels."

"But Mom, we always take showers. We can't go to bed without a shower."

"Tonight, you will have to. The sky won't fall if you don't shower. We are all tired. We can take them in the morning."

I had looked everywhere for towels because I wanted a shower too. I couldn't find them. The boxes were labeled and still no towels. I decided to clean up a little and air dry. Tomorrow, I would find the towels.

Morning arrived all too quickly, and Ted had to leave for his church appointments. The children and I were left to unpack and walk the neighborhood. But first, we had to find the towels. Again, I looked on the labels of each of the boxes. In the middle of the chaos, I found a laundry basket filled with dirty clothes.

Well that's not towels, but we do need laundry. I wonder if Grandpa hooked up the washer and dryer before he and Jim left yesterday.

Josh was only five, but he followed Grandpa everywhere. "Grandpa took the washer downstairs all by himself. Grandpa did it."

"Grandpa didn't do it all alone, did he?"

"No, some man helped him too."

"Well then, let's go down into the basement and see about the washer and dryer. Maybe they are connected and ready to go? I know just where the laundry soap is."

With Joni in her crib napping, Josh, Serenity, and I stepped carefully down the stairs into the basement. It was damp and musty, but the webs weren't as bad as I thought and soon we were finding special little hideouts and storage spaces.

I went up once to check on Joni and then headed down to start a load of laundry. When I opened the washing machine, I started to laugh.

"Josh and Serenity, come and see what mommy found. Let me lift you up to look in the washing machine."

I heard a chuckle from Josh and a squeal from Serenity. "The towels, the towels! We found the towels!"

"We can take showers now. But first, let's start a load of laundry."

Our journey as a pastor's family began with fond memories of the children and I playing together while their father was at work. We enjoyed the tree swing, the sandbox, and the walks around the block. The backyard was fenced in and the kitchen window was conveniently situated so that I could see the entire fenced-in area.

At night, we were often alone as Ted visited people in their homes or had meetings at church. We spent very little time as a family. I never asked where he went in the morning or what he did during the day. I assumed he was at church or making calls.

One morning, I received a phone call from the secretary at the church. "Is pastor there? He said he would be at the church by 9:00 a.m. and it is now ten thirty."

"I have no idea where he's gone. Possibly he is on a call."

"If you hear from him, would you have him call the church, please?"

"Of course. I am sorry."

"No need to be sorry. You are not the one who didn't show up at our scheduled time."

I didn't like the tone of her voice but pushed it aside and finished talking. I couldn't help but wonder where my husband, the pastor, had gone on such a beautiful day? He did not call but came home at approximately three in the afternoon. "Where have you been?" I asked. "Did you check in at the church? The secretary was calling for you."

"No, I didn't check in at the church. I decided to play eighteen holes with my dad. He happened to be in town and I couldn't resist golf on such a beautiful day. I don't have to be at the church every day."

"I took the call and am relaying the message. Please don't take it as an accusation."

We dropped the subject when he said, "I enjoy studying and preaching much more than I enjoy calling on people."

The call worried me. Mr. and Mrs. Patton were the patriarchs of the church, and I could sense dissatisfaction in their body language and their voice tone. I began to serve more in the church, thinking that would take eyes off Ted. The more I covered for him, the better ministry seemed to go. I couldn't call on people, but I opened our home to visitors from the church community. I stepped out of my comfort zone, and the congregation seemed pleased, not knowing the secrets I held behind closed doors.

Trouble in the Pastorate

Secrets that began to haunt me early in our marriage were not easily shaken nor shared. As Ted followed his desire to preach and play golf, my desire to cover for him became more intense. If all he wanted to do was preach, then I would lead the Sunday school program and follow through with youth group activities. This might keep everyone in check, at least for a while. But for how long?

When Mr. or Mrs. Paton called, I had a rehearsed answer. "I don't know where he is. Perhaps he went to see his parents."

"Don't you think you should know? He is your husband and the father of your children."

"Maybe, but I have never been in the habit of asking him where he is going."

"We think you should start. He is the pastor of the church, and we should be able to contact him."

I always agreed and then hung up as soon as possible without giving them any more reason for alarm. But they were alarmed. When their daughter, the secretary of the church, approached me about people who needed to be visited, I quickly changed the subject.

"What did you think of the Sunday school lesson? The children were on pins and needles as they learned about David and Goliath."

"I'm not questioning you, Lindsey. The lesson was terrific. I just want to know why Ted isn't making the calls the board requested, and I thought you might know."

"I think he is making some calls. Perhaps you should ask him about this?"

"We would, but so often he is not available to ask. I just thought you could give us more insight regarding this matter."

"I have told you what I know. It's time for me to take the children home, feed them, and get them down for naps. Thank you for your concern."

I carried a self-imposed responsibility to save face with others, keep the peace at church and at home, and to keep my husband employed. And always, the need to keep what happened in our home a secret. I began to focus more and more on the few teens in the church and isolate from the women that attended.

In the spring of the first year, the house we were living in was sold and we moved to the country, nearer to church and to closer scrutiny from the board members. If I hadn't felt pressure before, I certainly did now, even if Ted didn't seem to notice their watchful eyes.

I knew they were watching when one of the board members stopped by the house to see if he was home. I knew they were watching when I overheard complaints about his preaching. And I knew they were watching when they arranged for Ted and I to meet early on a summer morning to discuss something they felt was very important.

"As you know, the Christian school affiliated with our church is losing their administrator. We would like you to consider becoming the administrator of the school."

"That is a lot to ask, considering my role as your pastor."

"It would mean extra pay and the opportunity to supervise Joshua's education."

"I will have to think about it. The pay would be nice, but I am not sure I have the time."

"Do not think too long. We need to know. And, Lindsey, we asked you to this meeting for a specific reason."

I listened intently as they shared the need of the school for a lower elementary teacher.

"We are not asking you to teach for very long. You are much too busy with the children and your church activities. If you could just fill in until we find a new teacher."

"I would have Josh in my class. Would that be all right?"

"We've considered that and think it would be fine. Would you let us know by the end of the week? We need to get things settled at the school."

"Yes, I will give you my answer by Friday."

Ted told the board the following day that he would spend the next year as both pastor of the church and administrator of the school. It took me a little longer to decide, but by the end of that week, I did consent to taking the position.

Preparations began almost immediately. I had to prepare for school, but more importantly, I had to find someone to watch the girls. I did not have to search far. A kind and loving lady from the church volunteered to take the girls for the six weeks I taught school. Preparations for teaching were much easier than expected. I only had to prepare lesson plans. The extra activities, the bulletin boards, and the materials would all be ready when I entered the classroom.

When school began, so did the hectic schedule of balancing family, church activities, and school. I struggled with the responsibilities I thought were mine. No one had given me the tools needed to stop this incessant need to control the outcome of our family. When the six-week timeframe was nearing an end, I received a call from the chairman of the church board.

"We have found a teacher candidate for the open position at the school. We are just waiting for word on the background check."

"I enjoy teaching the class much more than I would have imagined. I have a teaching certificate and would like the opportunity to continue in this position."

"You have done a great job, but your responsibilities with the church are enough. We cannot expect you to teach as well."

"I want to teach. I love it. And Josh seems to like having his mother as his teacher. When he mistakenly calls me mom instead of Mrs. Jonson, the other students smile and he smiles as well."

"Other than waiting for the background check results, we are ready to hire this candidate. You should be able to stay home in approximately one week."

"Are you sure?"

"Yes, we are. Someone will let you know when she is starting."

It was difficult to finish the last week with enthusiasm and joy. I had looked forward to the days at school. To my surprise, our two daughters must have sensed the change in daily routine that was about to occur. They cried through breakfast, they did not want me to get them dressed, and where once they enjoyed going to the sitters, now it was a monumental task to get them into the car.

When a board member called to inform me that the permanent teacher would begin the following week, I was ready to stay home. The girls had convinced me that it was time. Neither of them were talking too much, but their actions spoke louder than words.

Being at home gave me the opportunity to watch planes come and go at the airport across the street. Home gave me the opportunity to watch ski divers floating beneath their parachutes. The girls and I were intrigued. The sun caused the various hues of reds and blues in the parachutes to sparkle and dance. The gracefulness with which the ski divers landed and their freedom to get back into the airplane to do it all over again were more than enough for us. We were hooked with watching, and I decided that one day I would jump out of an airplane. The open sky appeared to be a freedom I so longed for. Perhaps it would never come true, but I could dream.

While I taught school those first six weeks, Ted fulfilled his duties as administrator of the school and pastor of the church. He no longer had the freedom to play golf and have coffee with his friends. Every few days, one or more of the church board members popped in unannounced. My room was right next to the office and I could not help but notice.

Now I remained at home. I did not see when someone visited the school and I quite possibly lulled myself into thinking things were better between Ted and the church board. I wanted to believe it. But in late October when Ted arrived home and announced that he was playing golf, I was concerned.

"I don't like it. The weather is perfect for fall golf and I am in school. I think I will take the day off tomorrow."

"You will not. Someone is bound to find out."

"No one will know where I am. I am going out of town to play golf, and if anyone asks, tell them I am gone for the day."

"You know I cannot lie."

"You are not lying. You are telling the truth. I am gone for the day. You don't have to tell them why. Golf season is almost over."

Fortunately, no one asked me, and Ted reported more than once to the golf course in the following weeks. And although no one asked, eyes were watching. Controlling Ted was not something to be obtained, but they were certainly going to try.

Early in the winter of the following year, Ted began to talk of looking for a different church. As the board added more responsibilities, he saw the need to go somewhere else. He did not want this kind of pressure, and as it became more intense, I was not certain I liked it either. I finally consented to making another move.

Another Storm

Seven months after Ted announced his desire to find another pastorate, we arrived in Yorkville, Illinois. The seven months had passed by quickly. Ted searched for open churches, we visited the churches he thought would be a good fit, and finally he received a call.

We spent one weekend in Yorkville searching for a home to rent. Because the air traffic controllers were on strike, the homes they owned were being rented at a fraction of the cost. It was risky to rent a home that was on the market, but we decided to take that risk.

This particular home was in a subdivision outside of town and was immaculate inside and out. It was love at first sight, a dream come true. I did not even consider that the home could be sold. It would be ours while we lived in Yorkville; I just knew it. God would give me the desires of my heart.

As we turned into the driveway on that warm, sunny day in July, there was no disappointment. The house was exactly as I remembered. It looked even more inviting with a beautifully groomed yard. I couldn't wait to unpack and get settled. But first, there was something I just had to do. I had noticed the swimming pool when we decided to rent the home. It was cold and dreary then, but today, that was not the case.

Ted must have noticed me eyeing the pool from a distance. I was surprised when he said, "Walk down and find out how much it would cost. Maybe you and the children can join."

"Are you certain? I know you don't like to swim."

"Yes. I am guessing the children would enjoy the pool as much as they enjoyed watching the airplanes and sky divers at the airport."

This just was not like Ted, and although we had a U-Haul to unload, I decided to seize the opportunity. The U-Haul could wait for just a few minutes. As I returned from the pool, two cars pulled into the driveway. My thoughts returned to Michigan and the visits Ted received so often from the board. But these were not visitors checking on Ted. These were board members who had come to help unload the U-Haul. What a pleasant surprise. Someone to help, not question.

With the help of two board members and their wives, the U-Haul was unpacked in no time. The children stayed close, but soon, they were following one of the women around, checking out the playground equipment that remained in the yard. As night fell, dinner mysteriously appeared, and when bedtime rolled around, the children's beds were assembled and fitted with sheets. I had found their pajamas and they had found some of their toys. We were on cloud nine.

The following day dawned hot and sticky. Ted was leaving to meet the guys who helped us unpack, but just before he left, he handed me enough money to go down to the pool for the afternoon.

"If the kids like it, you can join for the summer."

"Are you sure? You can always join us if you have time."

"No thanks, but you have fun."

I unpacked another box or two of clothes, and after I found bathing suits, we headed down to the pool. We would spend many afternoons there during the rest of that summer.

Change of location does not change a person, and we were no exception. I continued to monitor Ted and the calls he made on members of the church. I had no way of knowing how to change in that area. No one had given me any tools, and even if they had, I may not have listened. I had been told for so long that something was wrong with me, so long that I believed it from the very depths of my soul. I was the problem. I had always been the problem.

Nothing about Ted changed either. He continued to play golf when the weather was good. He had an office but was not there when the board members called on him or when others wanted to meet with him. He was ill equipped to shepherd in the home or in the church.

I taught Sunday school, assisted in youth camps, and led Bible studies. I answered the phone and made excuses for my husband. I tried desperately to hang onto a church that provided an income for my children. But the church in Yorkville was not mine to hang onto. That was between God and my husband.

The women who helped me unpack called often, and we became friends. Not friends I risked confiding in, but friends who enjoyed having coffee and friends who would watch the children if I had an appointment. They were also friends who had wisdom beyond their years.

Although I did not confide in them, they apparently observed what I thought was so well hidden. Just a sampling of their comments showed evidence of this knowledge.

"Lindsey, we will watch the children if you can convince Ted to go on a date night."

"Lindsey, if you do not think you can confide in us, will you please find someone you can confide in? You need to talk to someone."

"We are here to help you, not hurt you. If there is anything we can do, please call. We cannot help if we do not know."

Comments such as these showed how much they cared, but I did not act on them. I intended to keep my world as private as possible. The secrets that had been kept for so long would continue.

Almost one year passed, and I lulled myself into believing that Ted would be pastoring this church for a very long time. I couldn't imagine it to be different. Thus, when Ted arrived home and announced he had a special meeting with the church board members, I was in disbelief.

The day of the meeting, I paced the hallways of our home, entering each room along the way, picking up any little thing that was out of place. Although my life felt totally out of control, my home would not be. Keeping it spotless gave me the illusion of control. If all was chaos, our home would not be.

Ted returned from that meeting not at all discouraged. "Nothing to be concerned about. It was just a reminder to fulfill my responsibilities at the church."

"That is not something to be concerned about? What are you going to do?"

"I am just going to do what I have been doing. Possibly I will make a few more calls on church members."

"Is that all? Are you going to be at your office during scheduled office hours? Are you going to write down in a notebook whom you visit and when you visit?"

"They did not say I needed to do that. You're the one who thinks I should write down whom I visit."

"But I want to stay here. I love Yorkville. Please do something?"

Ted did not do anything differently after this meeting, and I continued to live in a state of suspense, wondering when the board would call again. That did not happen. Instead, we received another phone call, a phone call I never expected.

When the phone rang, I picked it up. It was our landlord and his voice was exuberant.

"The house has sold. Not good news for you, but great news for us. This period of time has been so stressful trying to pay two mortgages. You helped some, but we were left with the bulk of the payments."

He rambled on until I had enough time to gather my thoughts.

"How long do we have before we have to move?"

"They would like to take possession in one month. I will try to hold them off a little longer, but their desire is to move in as quickly as possible."

I hung up the phone in sheer panic. One month to find another place to live, three children to consider in this move, and not enough income to be too choosy about another rental. I fell to my knees, not knowing whether to scream or cry.

Hadn't I been in this same situation many times before? Hadn't we moved enough times in our marriage? I must be the problem.

Possibly, I loved this home too much. I tried to call Ted, but there was no answer. He would have to wait.

I turned to thoughts of a home to rent. The paper was on the counter, and I started searching. When Ted arrived home, I turned to him in despair, but he was of little comfort.

"This doesn't have to done today or even tomorrow. We can start looking next week."

"That will leave us only three weeks. That doesn't seem like much time to find a place, pack, and get moved."

"It will all get done, and we will be moved before the month is over."

I wasn't so certain. Possibly I didn't trust enough, but taking action seemed the right way to go. While Ted had his usual coffee with one of the board members who helped us move, I found some leads and a realtor who might help us find a place to rent.

During the next few days, I contacted as many rental properties as possible, met the realtor, and determined a plan of action. The realtor was kind and considerate, but not very encouraging.

"There just are not many rental properties available right now. Are you sure you don't want to purchase?"

"No, we want to rent. There has to be something."

"I have found a few. I will help by setting up appointments so we can go see them. I'll call when I have these appointments set."

"Thanks. How can I say thanks?"

"You just did. I will talk to you early next week."

We looked at three homes the following week. None were suitable for our family. At the very beginning of the third week, our landlord called letting me know that we would need to be out in two weeks.

"I know how difficult this must be. We are praying. Have you found anything yet?"

"We have not found anything."

"Are you okay? I know this housing situation has put you under a lot of stress."

"Yes, I'm fine. Thank you for calling."

I hung up the phone and from the deepest place in my soul came a hysterical laugh. Was this some trick God was playing on me? Was I dreaming or was this actually happening? I pinched myself as the laughing stopped and the tears started flowing.

And that afternoon, I received another phone call, this time from the realtor who was helping us search for rental property.

"I received a call from a couple living in a farmhouse south of town. They are moving out one day prior to your move in date. That is cutting it close, but it sounds as if the house would be suitable."

"Are they willing to rent to a family?"

"They hesitated, but under the circumstances said yes."

"When can we see the house and how much is the rent?"

"The rent is slightly higher than you budgeted, but we haven't found anything in your price range and I do not think you will. As far as seeing the house, they are flexible. They would prefer that you come during the day and they would like to know two hours in advance."

We saw the home the following day, rented it, and were ready to move in on Saturday of the following week. We were far from the pool, but the home had a large enclosed front porch and a huge yard. The children would enjoy running and playing in the country.

It took a few weeks to get settled into our new home, but the time passed quickly. I painted a few walls and cleaned where it had been cleaned and then I cleaned where it didn't appear to have been cleaned. I hung pictures and enjoyed getting to know all the peculiarities of this country farmhouse.

After our move, I relinquished a few of my duties as a pastor's wife desiring to spend more time with the children before they started school in the fall. We climbed on the hay bales in the barn, we twisted and turned on the tire swing, and we cuddled with the kittens that frequented our front porch.

But this extra time, this relaxed state of mind was short-lived. When I learned of a special congregational meeting being held the following Wednesday at the church, I could no longer relax. My heart felt as if it skipped a beat, possibly three or four beats, and my mind began to race. There had been no talk of this meeting, yet I rationalized that I had not been around as much either. Was this meeting about Ted or about Sunday school? Just what could be so important that the board would call a special meeting? I would have to wait to find out because no one was talking.

The night of the meeting I drove to church alone, fingers clenched around the steering wheel, lips raw from biting them. I tried to turn off the committee in my head, but it was to no avail. I drove slowly, trying to prolong whatever it was that lay ahead. But driving slowly did not keep my mind from running wild, nor did it keep me from arriving on time.

As I entered the church, I found it strange that no one spoke to me, not even the two women who had become my friends. Something was terribly wrong. I was trembling as I contemplated running. Could I escape from what lay ahead?

When everyone was seated, we sang a few songs and then one of the leaders came forward and shared the board's vision for the church. Finally, the rest of the church board walked to the front and began to present information relative to the purpose of this meeting. They shared their desire for a strong pastor, a pastor who followed the guidelines that had been set in order to promote church growth. My head was spinning as they continued to talk.

I was sitting on the right side of the church, about three rows from the front, and from my vantage point I could see everything including Ted. His face was as white as a ghost and he had not moved a muscle since the board members began to speak. A portion of me wanted to run to him, to defend him, but the other part of me knew the board was right. Confusion and fear kept me glued to my seat. The board had presented their thoughts. Now how would they proceed?

It was a warm day, but I shivered as I vaguely heard one of the board members ask the members of the church to vote regarding the dismissal of their pastor. I wanted to scream, "That isn't right! That isn't fair," but I had no say in the matter. Ted was at everyone's mercy, and because I was his wife, I was at their mercy as well.

My mind was once again in overdrive. If only I had persisted with the girls in the teen youth group? If I had just prolonged resigning as the Sunday school superintendent until summer was over? If only, if only, if only.

When the board members finished counting the votes, Ted was asked to resign. A resignation on his resume was much more palatable than being fired. To make the resignation more inviting, the board offered him six-month's severance pay.

"Much more than we should ever offer. But when we considered how far you have moved with your family, and the time it will take to find a new church, we thought it only fair."

Ted had only one reasonable choice. That was to resign.

I tried to leave the meeting as unnoticed as possible. No one had talked to me before the meeting, and I did not want to talk to anyone now. I wanted to escape. I wanted to run from the hopelessness of my circumstances. I wanted this night and everything else to be over.

The women who had become my friends approached as I was opening my car door. They had been told they could not talk before the meeting. But this was not before; this was after.

"We want you to know how sorry we are."

"We want you to know this is not your fault. It has nothing to do with you."

"We love you and wish you could stay."

I heard but did not respond. The tears were so close to tumbling down my cheeks, and I did not want anyone to see my raw emotions. I trusted no one with my anguish.

"We are coming over, not tonight, but possibly tomorrow. You cannot keep us away."

"No, but I can lock the doors, so you cannot come in."

And with that said, I slammed the car door shut and quickly locked it. I considered the locked doors in my past and made a valiant attempt to switch off those thoughts. Now I had to focus on getting home.

I was the first to arrive. I checked on the children, paid the baby sitter, and climbed the stairs to the bedroom. I wanted to escape, to be rid of the pain that was tearing at every fiber of my being. Suicidal thoughts continued to surface, and tonight was no different. How could my life have become so hopeless? How could I even consider taking my own life?

Calm after the Storm

The stress of the congregational meeting weighed heavily on sleep. The blankets and sheets on the bed were a tangled mess, and the pillows were on the floor. Ted was nowhere to be found. My stomach did flip-flops as I thought of the decision made at the meeting. When I heard the doorbell ring, I jumped. Who would be here this early? And then I remembered the promise my friends had made after the meeting.

The window offered a perfect view of the driveway, and the car outside was definitely one of theirs. I hesitated but then grabbed my clothes and started dressing. They were ringing the bell a second and even a third time before I had dressed. I waited, thinking they would go away, but they were persistent. Evidently, their hearts were breaking as much as mine. I finally conceded, and as I unlocked the door, they burst through with arms open wide. The tears fell freely.

"Lindsey, in two weeks we are going to Naperville for a one-day women's conference. We have a ticket for you."

"There is no way."

"Yes, there is a way. We think it might be the most important thing you do while you are still in Yorkville. Please at least consider it."

"I am not going."

"We can wait, and your ticket will be waiting for you."

After several phone calls and another visit, my friends convinced me to go to the conference. The speaker was a therapist who seemed to have the ability to see through people. She certainly saw through me. She spoke about many of the issues that were plaguing me, and although she could not fix me, she did leave me with the opportunity to seek professional help.

The following morning, I called the number she had given me, and within three days, I was at my first appointment. Although I listened much more than I spoke, she seemed to comprehend, and the door was opened to future sessions.

After his resignation, Ted considered his best course of action. He deemed it necessary to play golf for relaxation. After all, for six months, he would have an income and that was certainly enough time to find a church. I nagged, and he didn't respond. I cried, and he only played golf more. The only course of action was to trust.

I made a valiant attempt at that, while Ted once again searched for open churches. We visited a few churches during the next five months, but he did not receive calls to pastor these churches. He finally took a job in the carpet industry, knowing his severance pay was coming to an end.

One of the few churches we had visited during the five months was a church in Michigan. We had heard nothing and had finally accepted the fact that this church had turned him down as well. But six weeks after taking his current job, he received a call to the church in Michigan. There was no question in his mind. We were going.

The children finished the school year, and with apprehension, I packed our things and said goodbye to my friends in Yorkville. I had opened a new chapter in my life. I had shared a few of the secrets that had kept me in my own prison. And now I had no choice but to leave.

I had one final session with my therapist. I listened intently as she tried to put some type of closure on our sessions together.

"First, I want you to find a therapist in Michigan as soon as you arrive. It is vital for your survival."

"I will. I promise."

"Second, you are not the problem in this marriage. I know you believe you are, but that is just not true. You are a very big part of the solution."

Her eyes pierced mine as she made her final comment.

"You know I have met with Ted once and that was with your permission. That one session gave me more insight into your marriage than all of our sessions combined. He told me that he did not need help, that you were the problem."

In desperation, I cried out, "I am the problem."

"No, that is what you believe. But you are not. His refusal to seek any type of help tells me he is the problem. You are being abused and have so accustomed yourself to this life that you know nothing different. Please continue getting help when you arrive in Michigan."

The tears trickled down my cheeks as we hugged and said good-bye. I left her office with a new word on my tongue. *Abuse*, what did she mean by abuse? Ted had not hit me, nor had he slapped me. There were no bruises on my body. But for the first time, I had heard the word *abuse* in the context of my marriage. It was something I would have to ponder for a very long time.

Just before moving to Ludington, I traveled there a second time to interview for a position at a newly organized Christian school. Taking the position opened the door to reinstating my teaching certificate and adding a masters' degree to my credentials. It also gave me something to look forward to when moving to a town where I knew no one.

When I finally arrived in Ludington though, I found I did not need something to look forward to. The location offered the children and me a beautiful beach and sunsets that filled the sky with oranges, yellows, and pinks. We were mesmerized by those sunsets, we hiked in the Ludington State Park, we went swimming, and we played in the sand.

The summer days were long and inviting, but most nights I tossed and turned. I could not rid myself of the never-ending thoughts of suicide that wreaked havoc in my mind. God would never forgive me if I got divorced, but suicide? I had found a verse, Romans 8:38, that I reasoned assured me of heaven even if I committed suicide.

I have no recollection of what finally pushed me over the edge that evening during our first summer in Ludington, but I was prepared and the opportunity arose. Ted was always out late, and I had no reason to believe he wouldn't be that night. I waited until I was certain the children were sleeping and then I attempted what I had planned for so long.

But God had plans for me, plans that were much different than I would have dreamed. Ted for some reason came home early that night and found me in a semiconscious state. The evidence of what I had done was on the floor beside me, and when he began to shake me, I regained enough consciousness to lash out in anger. I kicked and hit. I wanted to be dead. How could he come home early on that particular night? How dare he? After a short hospital visit and time with a therapist, I was allowed to go home. Yes, I promised I would make an appointment with her, but I never did. I was the problem and I did not need anyone else to confirm what I already knew.

While I played with our children, Ted got involved with the youth group at the church. Our home was soon bustling with teenagers. As I observed, I became aware of a need in the girl's lives. They desperately wanted someone to listen to them, and although I had just moved, although I had tried to commit suicide, I was that someone.

That fall, my teaching position, my ministry to the girls, and my own schooling left me juggling many hats. These were not hats I envisioned members of the church placing on me. Instead, they were hats I believed God had entrusted to me. In Ted's estimation, I continued to be the problem in our marriage, but in ministry, I became a solution. I could listen.

The teenage girls learned quickly they could trust me. After all, I kept my own secrets very well. Shortly after I began meeting with them, a first-time visitor approached me after the church service.

She said, "I think I can trust you."

"You can trust me."

That was the end of our conversation, but the following week, she sat next to me in church. Once again, she approached me.

"I found out you are the pastor's wife, but I still think I can trust you."

"Yes, I am the pastor's wife, and yes, you can trust me. It appears that you need to trust someone. And what is your name?"

"Savanah, and I do need to trust someone. Can we get together?"

Savanah and I started meeting on a regular basis, and it did not take long for me to recognize that her life paralleled mine in many ways. But the truth when revealed showed a much deeper level of abuse. Her husband had held a gun to her head on more than one occasion. One afternoon, Savanah said, "I have been told over and over again that I have to stay in this marriage. That's what God wants."

"Yes, that is His best plan, but not always the plan He has for us. He would not want anyone to suffer that kind of abuse. He is a loving God."

The words slipped off my tongue so effortlessly. How could I say that when I did not believe it? Could He possibly love her unconditionally and not me? Did the abuse that she lived with allow her the privilege of divorce? Just for today I had to listen, accept, and love Savanah. I could not, nor would I judge.

It took her almost two years to muster up the courage to file for divorce. During those two years, we walked and talked over and over again. I continued to affirm her and allow her to make her own decisions. She came to believe that her God was a loving God, and when her second husband passed away unexpectedly, she continued to live in the truth of God's love.

And what about the church Ted was pastoring? The church began to grow under Ted's leadership. Approximately eighteen months after we arrived in Ludington, the congregation came together for a meeting, a much different type of meeting than the one in Yorkville. They met as families to break ground for a church building. I wanted to believe we were in a spot that we could call home. The church building was evidence of a successful ministry. Or was it?

Growth in the church seemed to capitalize more and more on the teens in the area, and teenagers do not pay bills that occur with a building project. The desire Ted had to work with teens coupled with his desire to play the golf courses in northern Michigan caused friction in the church.

To ease the friction, I did what I knew best to do. I added to my already heavy load of responsibilities the task of being the Sunday school superintendent. I would make sure Ted did not lose his position at the church. But once again, Ted's position at the church was not mine to keep.

Nothing in our marriage changed, nothing about Ted changed, and without professional help, I did not change either. I walked the Ludington pier out to the lighthouse on a daily basis to escape the pain that was slowly engulfing me. Thoughts of suicide returned. But still, I did not seek help.

Late one Sunday evening, Ted walked in after a youth group meeting and said, "Tonight, the teens watched an X-rated movie during youth group."

"They did what?"

"One of the kids brought an X-Rated movie to youth group. I looked at the cover and didn't think it was too bad, so I let them watch it."

"What were you thinking? An X-rated movie."

"Some have watched this movie at home."

"Yes, maybe so, but not at church. Not in youth group!"

"No one will ever know. The kids will not say anything."

"You are wrong! Someone will find out."

It took a few short weeks for one of the board members to show up on our doorstep. I received the call that he was coming, and Ted opened the door. I couldn't help but hear the conversation that took place, and before he left, I knew what I had to do.

I went to bed knowing I had to leave this marriage. I no longer had to stay because I had the title of pastor's wife. That would soon be over. I no longer thought I had to stay because divorce was not acceptable. It simply did not matter. I was once again drowning in a sea of hopelessness, and this time I had to leave before it was too late.

It took two long months to devise a plan, a plan that would involve trusting others, something I had never mastered. I had no idea if Ted would fight for custody of the children, but I knew I needed to have custody during the week. There had been far too many absences in school this past year. I got them ready for school before I left, but they were not going to school. This had to stop, and it would be my responsibility to do so.

We lived in Mason County, and I feared trusting a lawyer from this county. I wanted a change of venue, and in order to do that, I had to take the children out of county for ten days. That is where trust came into play. I needed help.

After agonizing over this decision, I decided to ask for assistance from two women in the church. I reasoned they would be supportive due to recent circumstances at the church. Everything was going as planned until I received a visitor at school. I had no idea who he was, but when he handed me an envelope and asked me to sit down, I argued.

"Just tell me what this is?"

"Please sit down and then open it. I am here to serve you papers. You are Lindsey Jonson, aren't you?"

"What papers?"

"I am sorry that I have to do this. Your husband has filed, and I have been paid to be the messenger."

"I still do not understand. What is happening?"

"Your husband has filed. You will have to read the paperwork to find out, but I would advise that you locate a good lawyer. Again, I am sorry."

I still did not comprehend what was happening, but I had to get back to my children. My principal had watched them long enough. I swallowed hard and entered the classroom, determined to finish the day.

I left school that day totally confused. Nothing made sense. Ted would never file for divorce, and yet he had served papers. Why? I drove around Ludington and finally ended up at the beach. I sat in the car and carefully read the papers. Finally, I understood. The papers were not divorce papers, but papers that needed to be signed for a legal separation to take place.

As I began to walk out to the lighthouse, the question once again popped into my head. Why did he file for legal separation?

And the timing. Why now? I closed my eyes for just a moment and then it became clear. Ted had found out what I was doing, and he did not want me to have custody of the children. One of the women I had asked to help must have told him my plans.

My head began to pound as I realized the ramifications of what he had done. I could not take the children to another county. I had to stay in the house until this was settled. Fear gripped me. Never again would I trust someone to keep my confidence.

True Friends

Almost two weeks from the day I signed the papers, I received a call from my school administrator. "Will you please meet me in the office after school tomorrow afternoon? I need to talk to you about something."

I walked into his office the following day, burdened by the events happening at home. I had been silent about Ted's decision to file and now it was time to share that secret. I did not know what this meeting was about, but I knew my secret had to be on the agenda.

My principal started. "I asked you to come in so I could talk to you face to face. One of our board members heard a rumor that you were getting divorced."

I responded in disbelief. "That's not exactly true. Ted has filed for legal separation and I have signed the papers."

"Are you going to reconcile?"

I did not want to disclose how long I had been waiting for this moment. I simply said, "No, I am not!"

"Either way the school board feels you are no longer a good role model for our students. You are a wonderful teacher and a mentor to your peers, but you will not be able to teach here next year."

I sat silent, trying desperately to hold back the sobs.

"I want you to finish the school year. There are only two weeks left and then you will have two weeks to pack your things, finish your paperwork, and finally turn in your keys. I wish things were different, but there is nothing I can do."

He reached out to hug me, but I quickly withdrew to the other side of the room. I did not want him to see the tears forming in my eyes or my trembling hands. He must not know how badly I am hurting.

He followed me out of his office and down to my room. He reached out once more, but this time with information to share.

"I know of two wonderful counselors in Grand Rapids that you might consider calling. I know their sessions are free and I have a feeling that you may need some good, free counseling. Let me know if there is anything I can do."

He walked out of the room and left me to face the fear that was forming inside me. I stifled the sobs that were beginning to erupt from the core of my being. How could this happen so quickly? Was God already punishing me for even thinking about divorce? I wanted to escape the room and drive to the lake. I needed to walk, to escape the feelings of abandonment and rejection. First the church body, now the school. Who next?

The next two weeks became a blur as I prepared for the final week of school, began to clear out my possessions from the classroom, and searched for a lawyer. Denial would not make my circumstances disappear, and I had to be prepared for whatever my future held. At times I thanked God for Ted's decision to file. Although he would not file for divorce, he had given me the momentum I needed to move forward, and it was now up to me to keep that momentum going.

I stumbled upon a lawyer from another county, and he proved to be perfect. He encouraged me to ask for what I rightfully should have, and he did not push me to file for divorce. However, at one point during the summer, he filled out the divorce papers.

"This will allow you to file without paying for another appointment. That is, if you decide to file."

After the judge granted me partial custody of the children, he encouraged me to talk to Ted. Fear of repercussion kept me from engaging in any type of conversation with him, and my lawyer felt it important that I attempt to take a step in that direction. In retrospect, I believe I feared that God would make me go back much more than I feared Ted.

We met on a cold sunny day in October. I was already living in my own apartment and had not seen Ted since the custody hearing. I arrived first and seated myself across from my lawyer, with a vantage point of the office door. Immediately upon his arrival, I moved to sit next to my lawyer. Ted began the session and his berating continued until my lawyer closed the session forty-five minutes later.

When Ted left the room, my lawyer turned to me. "He just spent forty-five minutes berating and abusing you, and you did not say a word. Are you ready to sign the divorce papers now?"

I signed that afternoon, and the process began to finalize the divorce. I had taken a new part-time teaching position in Scottville, Michigan. I asked for very little in the divorce proceedings, so I also worked at a local deli in the area. I prayed for the day when my teaching position would pay the rent and support my children.

I also prayed for the day I would not live in fear that God would make me go back into a marriage I so desperately needed to escape. When my pickup truck broke down, I knew that God was punishing me for filing. When I had to move because I lived in subsidized housing and my income increased beyond their limit, I knew God was going to make me go back.

I lived in isolation and fear, surrounding myself with my children and their friends who frequented our apartment. They seemed safe when no adults had proven themselves safe. But I would soon begin to see the fallacies of my belief system. In early summer of the following year, a couple, parents of children I had in my previous classroom, appeared on my front doorstep. She wanted to hang out with my girls while her husband took me on a motorcycle ride.

I enjoyed their company on more than one occasion, and in early August, the tables were turned. I called them and asked if they would give me a ride from down state back to my home. I had purchased a motorcycle and didn't know how to ride it. The stammers and stutters from across the phone wires brought laughter to my heart. I reasoned that they could teach me how to ride until I could get into the state motorcycle course. They were delighted to do that as long as the motorcycle stayed at their house until I appeared comfortable on it.

I quickly agreed, and before the motorcycle had to be stored for the winter, I learned to ride. I also learned there were people I could trust, a refreshing thought for someone who feared trusting anyone.

The year ahead held no chaos. In fact, I finally did get a full-time teaching job with a salary that paid the rent and supported the children. I felt that quite possibly, God was on my side. I continued to live with the demons that invaded my mind about returning to Ted, but I also lived with some semblance of peace until that fateful night almost one year later.

Raped

"It wasn't the walk," I later rationalized. "It was the unseen danger that was lurking around the corner." The evening stars were enchanting. They were already beginning to sparkle when I arrived home from work, and now as I put on my tennis shoes and stepped out for my usual walk, I couldn't help but smile. Fresh air caused my lungs to explode as I inhaled and exhaled with every step. The thought of danger never entered my mind.

One short hour later with the enticement of a hot shower just around the corner, I turned the key in the lock and stepped into the quiet space I called home. In the past I felt unsettled and chaotic, never knowing when and if I would have to move. Now I allowed myself the luxury of relaxing. I was in control of where I lived, no one else.

After showering, I wrapped myself in an oversize bathrobe and sat down to sip a mug of hot chocolate with marshmallows. The aroma of the chocolate, the sweetness of the melting marshmallows, and the quietness of my apartment left me in a relaxed state—a perfect time to meditate and journal.

Just as I began to pen my thoughts, the doorbell rang. *Who could it be?* I wondered as I rose to open the door. I looked through the peephole and recognized the man on the other side as the parent of a little girl in my school. Without another thought, I opened the door.

He spoke briefly as he slammed the door and turned the deadbolt. "You must be here to talk about your daughter," I said. In retrospect, I wonder why that thought even entered my mind at eight thirty. He had not come to talk but to carry out what he had been planning to do for more than six months.

His actions were direct and bold, and all the fighting and screaming only made him more intent on keeping me quiet and hurting me more. Nothing I did could stop him, and at some point, I slipped into survival mode. As I wept, the repulsion and violation I felt turned into rage and from my innermost being I cried, "You will survive. You will survive."

At that moment, I must have blacked out. When my eyes opened, they opened to an empty apartment. The aroma of hot chocolate no longer filled the air. Instead, the stench of his body permeated the room, confusion reigned, and I ached all over. I was alive, violated, and hurt, but I was alive.

I crawled to the phone, too weak to stand, and pulled the phone book from the shelf. In the Yellow Pages I found the number of the Women's Crisis Center. I dialed and immediately the phone was answered with a recorded greeting. As I began to sob, someone picked up and tried to talk to me. I couldn't answer. Through the uncontrollable sobs, the words finally came out, "Someone raped me. Someone raped me."

As I regained strength, I began to sit up and look around my apartment. It was in disarray and almost surreal. I told myself over and over, "Do what the woman at the Crisis Center said to do." The very words seemed to help keep the focus on what I needed to do and not on what had just happened to me.

The woman on the other side of the phone had been very compassionate but also very firm in her directions. The most important thing she said was, "Do not take a shower or wash, and put any garments he may have touched in a grocery bag. Concrete evidence is crucial." I did not understand the ramifications of what she was saying, but I would later.

A hot shower was what I wanted most. It would somehow erase the degrading, awful feeling that was beginning to overwhelm me. I repeated the words, "Do what she told you to do, not what you want to do."

At that moment, I could not fathom calling the local police, but that was supposed to be my next step. I gazed around the apartment once again in disbelief. The committee in my head began to race. *You opened the door. You know these police officers, and you certainly don't want to tell them what just happened. The men in your life have abused and abandoned you. How do you know these officers will be any different?*

With that thought running through my mind, I somehow fell into a restless sleep, and when I finally gazed at the clock, over two hours had passed since that initial call. It was time to do something, anything. No more denial.

My body still ached, but the dizziness and confusion appeared to be subsiding. I took a few tentative steps. These steps gave me courage to drive myself to the hospital. I still had not called the police.

I couldn't imagine what the admitting staff saw when I entered the doors. Most knew me, and they looked astonished as the ER attendant wheeled me into the room. For the second time, I had to repeat the words that would haunt me for so very long. "I was raped."

Emergency room doctors exploded through the doors and nothing could have prepared me for the next step. They tried to be gentle, but they had to examine me, and as they did, I clenched my teeth and clung to the guard rails. The screams were on the tip of my tongue. I chewed violently on my lips, a childhood habit, and the tears streamed down my cheeks. By the time the doctor finished, my lips were bleeding, and the nurse was crying as she wiped my tears and soothed my lips with a cold compress. Then she proceeded to poke me again. "HIV is always an issue. We hope you didn't come in contact with any sexually transmitted diseases and this blood test will help us determine that. Your doctor will check again in six months."

The exam was over, but the reality check of calling the police still loomed ahead. Again, I resisted until one nurse said, "I have checked who is on duty, and Officer Crandall will be in at 6:00 a.m. It might be easier to talk to a female."

That was three hours away, an eternity away, but I knew in the depths of my heart that she was right. Somehow in three hours, I would have to gather the courage to say, "Someone raped me."

Will It Ever Be Over?

Shortly after six in the morning, Officer Crandall arrived. She recognized me immediately, and her eyes spoke volumes. I didn't have to make the call. She already knew. I stared into her eyes and tried to speak, but the words were caught in my throat. Finally, I cried out in despair, "I was raped."

Just as water descends and crashes over a waterfall, the details of the rape began to tumble and crash in random order. Officer Crandall sorted it out by asking question after question. The one she repeated most often was, "Why didn't you call right away?"

I reiterated what I had told the nurses in the emergency room. "I have been abused and rejected by men. Why would I trust a man now?" At some point after Officer Crandall finished questioning me, she stood at my bedside as I called my teenage daughters. They had been at their father's overnight and had to be told.

When the girls arrived at the hospital, they were confused and scared. They immediately wanted to know what was wrong. I was so grateful Officer Crandall had agreed to help me talk to them. As we told them what had happened, my daughters and I clung to each other. I know God was with me through the rape, but at that moment, He gathered us in His arms and comforted us as only He can do. His promise in Psalm 46:1 came to mind in those early morning hours. *"God is my refuge and strength, an ever-present help in trouble."*

The rest of the day was a blur. Somehow, the police entered my apartment for more evidence. Someone must have called my principal to inform him that I would not be at school. I knew my perpetrator, so the detectives were already doing a background check and gathering the information they needed to bring him in for questioning.

Before I left the hospital that afternoon, the detectives had gathered this much information. My perpetrator, a parent of a little girl in our school, had a name. I had failed to give it to Officer Crandall, and for some reason she never asked. Why? I don't know. Perhaps speaking his name made him more human, and right now, I considered him to be an animal.

When the detectives called to ask a few questions, I had to put a name with his face, a face I wanted to forget so badly. "Yes, his name is Ron Belmont." My stomach was in my throat as I repeated it. The detectives said, "Ron has had three priors, but the victims have only reported the rape. No one has prosecuted."

They continued, "When brought into custody, his parents have posted bail, and he is out in a day or two."

What I also learned was even more frightening. "His pattern has been to return," the detective at my bedside said. "Keep your doors locked at all times. We will watch your apartment closely, but be prepared to call 911 if he does."

I was in disbelief. I repeated the words. "What? You are telling me he could return?"

Fear gripped my body. Where would I go to be safe? I felt like a prisoner in my own home. His patterns were as predictable as mine had been. One week later, the doorbell rang. It was late in the evening. I looked through the peephole and was staring into the face of the man who had raped me. With an inaudible gasp, I ran to my daughter's room. It was as far away from the door as I could get, and there I made the call. Only then did I give way to the terror that was gripping my entire body. Burying my head in a pillow, I began to scream. In the short amount of time it took for the police to arrive, he had already disappeared.

Although this repeat appearance was terrifying, it put the police at a definite advantage. They could now expedite the warrant needed to arrest him. But first, they had to find him. This took place in the most unusual of circumstances.

I was a teacher in a school district with three small elementary buildings. My principal, Scott, was a teddy bear. He was firm but loving with the students, and he treated his staff in the same manner. He was an effective principal because he was well organized, and he cared.

He cared enough that after four days calling in sick, he was no longer satisfied with my excuses. He called my home. I hesitated as I picked up the phone. I had no caller ID. When I heard Scott's voice, I relaxed. He said, "Everyone loves you and misses you. Something is terribly wrong. You are never sick. Can you come in to see me this afternoon?" I had no choice. He would not accept my excuse of being sick any longer, not without seeing me.

That afternoon, I walked in and slumped down in one of the old green stuffy chairs that inhabited his office. Concern was written all over his face. I looked directly at him, desperately trying not to cry as he started asking questions. Finally, I pressed my hand to my ears as if to stop the questioning and then blurted out the words, "I was raped."

With tears streaming down his cheeks, he reached across the desk and grabbed my hands. "I will do whatever I can to help you. Anything, just ask." I didn't have to ask. Instead, within a week, the police asked for his help. They wanted Ron behind bars as soon as possible. They knew he would probably run, but not without his daughter. That's where Scott fit in.

Exit papers were needed in order for his daughter to be registered in another school, and Scott had already received the call for those papers. He knew exactly when Ron was coming into the office. He told the police, "I'll detain him until you arrive."

At approximately one thirty in the afternoon, Ron arrived at the school and Scott called him into his office. "Your daughter's exit papers will take just a few minutes longer," he said. As the door to his office closed, Scott's secretary called the police not knowing why but doing exactly as she had been told.

Time stood still as I watched the clock and waited for the phone to ring. When it did, I jumped. I wept as Scott said, "It's over. He is in custody." What I didn't realize even then was that it would never really be over.

Considering

Now that Ron was behind bars, I smiled a little more and was less irritable. I kept quoting 2 Corinthians 12:9: "My grace is enough. My strength comes into its own in your weakness." For a brief time, I knew His grace was enough. I was still missing too much school, and when I was in my apartment, the sights and smells that I remembered from that dreadful night haunted me. Although the reminders of that night were always present, God was also present as I read His word, as I worshipped Him in song, and as I basked in His creation. His strength kept me going.

His presence kept me going, but it did not keep me from missing school or leaving at noon. This happened frequently, and it did not take long for my peers to notice. They came to me with questions on more than one occasion and were not satisfied with my answer. One of the teachers said, "There has to be more. This just isn't you, Lindsey."

Finally, with the prompting and support of my principal, I decided to tell the staff. God gave me the courage as I sat in the staff lounge with Scott by my side and once again said, "I was raped." For a moment, it was as if time stood still. Then in one simultaneous move, the teachers gathered around me in love and support. I had been trying to deny the rape, not realizing that denial lengthened the pain and isolated me from the people that loved me. They were now my cheerleaders from the side. They prayed.

Being strong in God's grace empowered me with courage and strength as I entered the Mason County Courthouse to speak with Terry Cummings, the prosecuting attorney. Terry was kind and considerate, but very matter of fact. His dark brown eyes pierced mine.

His office was warm and stuffy and located on the second floor of the courthouse. A large table separated us, and the chairs were hard and uncomfortable. I sat across from him and listened intently. The meeting was brief. Terry provided me with details about what to expect the next time we met, and then asked one question. "You have reported. Do you want to prosecute?"

I knew that if I took no action, this man would be free to rape again. After some discussion, I agreed to meet him once more. This time he would be questioning me as if I were in the courtroom.

In Luke 1:37, I read, "Nothing is impossible with God." During the next two weeks, I made a valiant attempt to believe this was going to be possible, but every time I tried to imagine what Terry would ask, my lips began to quiver and tears filled my eyes. Sleep evaded me, and teaching school was next to impossible.

I rehearsed over and over the events of that evening. I questioned myself, *Why did you let him in? Why didn't you fight harder?*

I continued to hear Officer Crandall ask, "Why didn't you call the police right away?" I counted the days until I would meet with Terry again. I was terrified and couldn't sleep or eat. Scott arrived at school the morning of the meeting with Terry to find me pacing the hallways.

"I wanted to teach school. I insisted. I don't have to meet Terry until three this afternoon."

"You do not belong here today. Go home, put on your walking shoes, and walk. Find Al and walk with him."

I followed his orders and walked. I walked until my legs felt as if they would fall off, then showered and headed for the courthouse. The drive was barely ten minutes, but it seemed like forever. And being in that space where God's grace was empowering me somehow eluded me. I quickly stepped out of that space and into the role of a victim. I knew that role well for I played it most of my life.

But now was not the time to be a victim, it was the time to rise up and allow God's grace to carry me. That didn't happen. The victim, the little girl in me, was present when I finished walking, and she didn't leave when I entered Terry's office. I hung my head in shame as I listened and tried to answer his questions. The man who had been so gentle was now hurtful and fierce. I felt like I was being raped all over again, and in a sense, I was. Reliving the moments before, during, and after brought me to my knees.

"My tactic," he said, "is simple. This was to prepare you for the courtroom, if we go to court, and you really struggled. You have to be emotionally strong and prepared. The courtroom will be brutal, and I want you ready. Lindsey, we want this guy put away."

As I left his office, I pondered what Terry had said. "You really struggled. You have to be emotionally prepared." I questioned, *Am I prepared? Can I do this with God's help?"*

When I arrived home from the courthouse, my daughters were there to greet me. We embraced, not wanting to let go. The tears fell freely. Finally, I gathered the courage to whisper, "I can't do it. I am not going to prosecute."

Serenity, my oldest daughter, was the first to speak. "You have to, Mom. He will do it again and the next time it could be me."

I responded, "Terry told me I don't have to do anything, I don't have to do anything I don't want to do. It's my choice."

Without another word, I escaped to my room, grabbed my tennis shoes, and headed for the streets. I recalled vividly the words of our chief of police. "You are not to walk alone under any circumstances." However, at that moment, I didn't care. I walked.

I must have worn the soles of my tennis shoes down to nothing during the next four weeks. I cried at the drop of a hat and the voices in my head kept saying, *You cannot do this. You are not strong enough.* I allowed Serenity's words tangled with mine to wreak havoc with my emotions. I had made the decision, but why the confusion? Her words were so powerful. And if I did not come to a final decision soon, was I not giving up? No decision was giving up without saying the words.

I lived on this roller-coaster ride for two weeks. Late one afternoon, I received a phone call from the chief of police, a phone call that would make Serenity's words pierce my heart and the decision to prosecute much easier. His words echoed in my ears. "I have seen you walking alone, and it has to stop. Ron is out on bail."

Later, I would learn that his parents had bailed him out, but right then I just wanted the doors locked and the world shut out. I wanted all that had happened to go away. I wanted my daughters and myself safe. I wept in frustration and fear, not knowing where to turn. I knew that I could talk to God, but my words were always the same. "You have a plan, but I don't understand it. Please tell me what I need to do so bad things don't keep happening to me."

The Song

I had met with Terry twice, had told a select few people, and still the local newspaper had not printed the story. I pleaded with our local reporter. "Please keep it out of the news. I don't see any possible reason for the story to be publicized. It will just promote gossip and small talk, and I don't want to be asked questions right now." I felt guilty and ashamed, and I didn't want anyone else to know, but once again he had come to me, as if he had to ask.

"This story has to hit the news. If not for you, then for the safety of others in our community."

"There is no reason after this long. I just don't understand how publicizing the story will keep others safe. It's just a good story for you."

Although he was determined, I held my ground. I wanted it as private as possible, and although he didn't like it, he finally agreed. "The *Ludington Daily News* will have to do without this piece of news. You are not necessarily right, but you win this time."

Keeping my name out of the news gave me precious time to contemplate the trial without being questioned by people in the community. It also gave me time to keep a commitment I had made to the choir director at a local church. Three months earlier, she had asked, "Will you sing a solo portion in our church musical?"

I had agreed, and when I went to the first practice, I knew it was the perfect song. The pitch was perfect, the melody beautiful, and the words a picture of what I desired God to do for me. No one else appeared to have protected me, but as I reflected, I could see how God had protected me during so many stormy days. Now I wanted to sing this song for Him.

That was before I was raped. Now I wasn't at all sure. It had only been a few short weeks, and I hadn't had to testify yet. Still, I had made a commitment, and I was going to keep my word. I waited as long as possible to show up for practices. The director finally called. "You have to make it to the next practice. I need to hear you with the entire choir and I want to hear your solo piece. We are only two weeks out. Please be here tomorrow or I will have no option but to give the song to someone else."

I went to practice the following day knowing that I could not do this on my own but that God would be the one giving me the strength to sing. I watched the faces of those around me. I had no clue whether any news had reached the public ear. Then I turned my focus to the wall on the far side of the room. It worked, and I managed to get through practice. When we finished, the choir director asked, "You are not yourself. Are you sure you are all right?"

"I am fine. Just a little tired." I assured her that I would be stronger for the final practice. I was determined to sing this song.

Between this practice and the next, I had to reconcile my confused mind. I had to be satisfied with reporting the rape or to go ahead with prosecuting. Possibly I had made that decision already, but voicing it would somehow allow me to stay focused on the song. Possibly, my voice would be stronger. I could only hope.

Two meetings with Terry made me fully aware of how difficult a trial would be, but the final decision was made when Josh called to talk. He knew what had happened but had avoided the topic. Now he was vocal in his desire to put my perpetrator in prison. I responded rather abruptly. "How can you be so sure I can do this?"

"Mom, you can do it," was his response. "I know you can."

I called Terry the next morning to tell him to proceed with the prosecution. He already had enough evidence to put Ron in prison, but he warned me. "This will be a difficult one. Even with the evidence we have, there are some circumstances that might cause holes in the case." I heard his words but dismissed them as I focused on what was next. I have to sing a song about God's protection.

One more practice and the director said, "You do sound much stronger, and you are smiling a little. Now if you can just get a little of that glow back"

"I will do the best I can."

The following Sunday was sunny and warm. It was a breath of fresh air after the cold, rainy week we just experienced. My heart was encouraged, and I knew God had my back. But did I trust Him enough to sing about His protection when I did not feel like He had protected me? I arrived early and had time to sit and meditate. Thoughts raced through my head. Now that I had made the decision to allow Terry to prosecute, there was much to do. If the lawyer questioned me anything like the prosecuting attorney had questioned me, I was in trouble.

Focus, I said to myself. *Only one thing at a time.*

I refocused quickly when our director said, "It's time to go onstage. Everyone ready? Lindsey, are you all right?"

"I am fine. I will be fine."

As we walked on stage, I kept my eyes on the same wall that I had focused on during practice. The songs we sang as a group were not hard. I just had to keep my mind on the moment.

It was time for me to step out and sing. I hesitated and then gave the nod that I was ready. I really don't know how I made it through the song. The tears glistened on my cheeks as I sang about God's protection. I tried to focus on the wall, but the words were so real. Somehow, I couldn't fathom God's protection when I had just been raped. But I kept on singing, and when I finished, the crowd stood to their feet.

I quickly took my spot back in the choir. The tears were flowing harder now, and I had all I could do to keep my composure. When we were finished, I tried to leave quickly. The choir director found me and hugged me tightly as she said, "You were fantastic today, but something is wrong. I may not know what it is, but please call if you ever want to talk."

I didn't want to talk. I wanted to escape. I ran out to greet the early evening sky. The moon was beautiful and there were far too many stars to count. I looked up at them as if I were looking at God. These words escaped my lips. "God, I will never sing again." I drove home and found my Bible. I took it outside and tore it page by page into little shreds.

The anguish and hopelessness I felt at that moment were more than I thought I could handle. I looked up into the heavens and stared. Tears streamed down my cheeks as I recalled Psalm 56:8. "You keep track of all my sorrow. You have collected all my tears in your bottle. You have recorded each one in your book."

God, I have tried to follow you for as long as I can remember. But right now, it doesn't appear that you remembered to catch my tears in your bottle. My whole life has been tears. Do you really have them all in your bottle? Chaos and abuse are so much a part of my childhood and my marriage. And remember, he filed for separation first. Is this punishment for getting a divorce? You are taking care of five of my precious children in heaven. Do you have the tears I cried for them in your bottle also?

As I stepped from the dewy grass onto my doorstep, my thoughts and feelings were tearing my heart in two. "What is next, God?" I said. "If I continue to follow you, will I encounter more atrocities?" In that moment, I made a conscious decision to try life my way without obeying God.

Sentenced

I tackled the weeks before I would have to face Ron with my heart in torment, and my mind in constant motion. How will I get through this? Will Ron be convicted? If convicted, how long will he be in prison?

And finally, the question that haunted me the most. "What am I doing to his family?" My children heard me voice this concern and immediately came to the rescue. "You are not doing anything to him, Mom. He raped you and three other women before you. You are simply the first one with the courage to prosecute."

Every thought centered on life after rape and life before trial. The days were endless and the night hours agonizing. I tossed and turned, with my legs in constant motion. The journal by my bed was filled with what-ifs and things to be done. As slowly as the hours passed, the day of the next meeting arrived almost unnoticed. No doubt, I didn't forget. I accompanied Terry into a smaller room in the courthouse.

As we were sitting down, the other door opened. I gasped as the defense attorney entered the room. His face looked vaguely familiar. My mind raced. How do I know him? Why does he look so familiar? I tugged at Terry's' arm.

"Sit tight. We haven't even started."

"Yes, but we need to talk."

"We will. Right now, be patient."

Just then, Ron walked into the room and I no longer had the need to speak. My tongue was caught in the back of my throat. Tears welled in my eyes as I controlled the indescribable urge to run. The room was silent as Terry started to speak. When he was finished, the defense attorney called me to come forward. My legs trembled as I stood to my feet and walked tentatively to the stand.

After swearing to tell the truth, he began to question me. There were many questions, but the one question that will be etched in my mind forever would be the one that would end any further questioning.

"Ms. Jonson, how do you know that you were raped?"

I responded with a boldness I didn't think I had. "How do I know I was raped? I would know. My husband raped me when we were married."

"Why didn't you say that during the hearing for the custody of your children?"

"Who would have believed me? My husband was a pastor."

It seemed as if all eyes were on me as Terry stopped everything and asked me to step out. The room grew quiet. So quiet you could have heard a pin drop.

"Why didn't you tell me? Why didn't you say something?"

"I tried but you wouldn't let me. You said to be still."

"Yes, I did. I am sorry, but this could end up being to our advantage. Let's wait and see how it plays out." I wasn't sure what he meant, but I was willing to wait and glad for the reprieve however long it might be. Terry was called out of the room where we were waiting, and I stayed behind to chew my fingernails and bite my lips. I didn't have to wait long.

Terry hesitated as he entered the room. "They want to plea bargain. You may not like it, but please consider the offer."

"What is the offer? You haven't told me."

"Two years in prison and extended hours of community service."

"That's not enough. Not nearly enough."

"I agree, but he will have a record. If we go to trial, he may go free. He will now be labeled a sex offender."

"Two years just doesn't seem enough," I sobbed.

"Are you ready to answer more questions like the defense attorney just asked? And it will be a different attorney. A conviction on his record is so important. You did it, Lindsey."

It didn't seem nearly enough, but the thought of more questioning left me reeling. Everything would be over. Life would return to normal, at least that's what I told myself.

"Are you sure, Terry?"

"It is your decision but going to trial is risky. A trial could leave Ron walking away a free man. I cannot make the decision for you, but a conviction is more than I anticipated."

Reluctantly, I agreed, and Terry left the room once again to talk to the defense attorney. When he returned, my fists were clenched and my jaw tight.

"You will have to face the defense attorney and Ron one more time."

"Why?" I sobbed.

"You have to agree to their offer. One more time and then we can talk about what happened. You can do this. It's almost over."

I took a deep breath, wiped my eyes, and stood to my feet.

"I'm ready."

We stepped out of the room to face the defense attorney and my perpetrator. I gasped as I stared into the eyes of the man who had devastated my life. I finally gathered enough courage to speak.

"I accept your offer. I accept your plea bargain."

An officer was there to lead Ron away.

I was left to mull over all that had happened in the past months. Ron's sentence was two years. How long would mine be? Would this ever be over?

Amazing Grace

As I began to run from God, I also continued to walk with a special needs young man. Al struggled in school and also had some involuntary body movements. His life intertwined with mine very soon after I was raped. At that time, I had no choice but to walk with someone if I wanted to walk, and I so wanted—no, needed—to walk. We never walked at a snail's pace but rather challenged each other on every walk.

"It's hot today. Lindsey, do you think we can still walk three miles in forty minutes?"

"I'm always up to the challenge," I replied. "Let's go."

After many months of walking, Al challenged me with a different question. I never expected this question and wasn't prepared to answer.

"My mom said you used to pray. Why not now?"

"I am not praying anymore, and I don't have to give you more of an answer."

Al accepted the answer, and we continued to walk. On the hottest days, the longest walks left Al sweating and exhausted, but he never quit. We called each other the walking fools. At least one year passed before Al asked me another question. It wasn't lack of courage that stopped him, but most likely he was waiting for one that carried weight. When it finally happened, I again was caught off guard.

It seems that special needs children have a special gift, and Al's gift was music. He belonged to a band called the ABC's of Music. The band was making a CD, and Al was more than excited. He was bursting with enthusiasm and determination.

"Lindsey, I have to sing a very special song for the ABC's of Music. Will you help me learn the words?"

"What is the name of the song?"

"'Amazing Grace.' My mom said you would know the words."

"Your mom said I would know the words, did she?"

"Yes, she did. I know she's right. Will you please help me?"

"No, Al, I will not help you. I cannot."

"All you have to do is sing the song and record it. I can learn the words from the tape."

"I said no, and I will not change my mind."

Less than one week passed before Al posed the same question. My answer must have been less convincing. The following day when I arrived for our afternoon walk, Al met me at the car with tape recorder in hand. His voice was confident as he spoke. "Lindsey, you are the only one who can help me. Please, you have to."

My heart may not have been soft to God, but it was soft to Al. And without giving it another thought, I gave Al my final answer. Just a little less than two years prior, I told God I would never sing again, and the following day, I sang "Amazing Grace" into Al's tape recorder.

There were no tears. There was not a hint of recognition that I had made a baby step into recovery, but God has a plan, and Al was an important part of that plan.

At the Marina

Several months after I sang "Amazing Grace," Al came to me with a second request.

"My mom is going out of town in July, and I will not have anyone to take me to church. Will you take me?"

"You know the answer to that question, Al. I don't go to church."

"I know you don't go now, but you used to go. You can take me if you want to."

"No, you are wrong. I have not gone in a very long time, and I don't intend to start now. I will not take you."

"Please will you pray about it?"

"Al, I don't sing, I don't pray, and I certainly don't go to church."

"You did sing 'Amazing Grace,' so I am going to pray that you take me to the marina for church."

"Go ahead and pray. I am not taking you to church."

I thought that would be the end of the discussion, but after another week of walking, Al approached me once more.

"Please, Lindsey, I want to go. Church is at the Ludington Marina. You don't even have to go inside."

"What if it rains?"

"If it rains, we won't go. You can stay home or we can walk in the rain."

"Are you sure? We won't go if it is raining."

"Yes, I promise."

My heart softened, as it always did with Al, and after our next walk, I found myself agreeing to take him to church at the marina. As soon as the words slipped out, I tried to take them back. I couldn't believe I had agreed to such a ridiculous request. Al knew I didn't go to church and he still had persisted. Now I had to go.

Although I had just finished telling Al I didn't pray, for the next two weeks, I prayed diligently for rain. I didn't pray for just any rain; I prayed for a drenching on the Sunday I was to take Al to the marina. I walked and prayed, I slept and prayed, and I even showered and prayed, all in hopes that God would miraculously hear and answer my prayer.

Two weeks passed quickly. I didn't remotely believe God would hear me, but when I woke up on Sunday morning, I was pleasantly surprised. *Tap, tap, tap.* Was that rain on the roof? *Tap, tap, tap.* I heard it again. I quickly stood up and walked to the window. It was rain and it appeared to be a slow, steady, all-day rain. My heart began to race. Did God answer my prayer? Would the church service be canceled? I would have to wait and see.

I grabbed a pair of pants and a T-shirt and pulled them on as I ran for the door. The thoughts dancing in my head didn't have anything to do with the rain or the possible cancellation of the church service. Those thoughts centered on the possibility that God had heard me when I prayed. It had been a very long time since I had given God the opportunity to listen to my prayer. I hadn't prayed.

Now I was thanking Him as I backed out of the driveway and drove to the Ludington State Park. It was time for a good hike, a hot shower, and a breakfast of champions when this was accomplished. What a great start to the day.

I hiked the trails in amazement that God might be answering my prayers. Once I thought the sky seemed to be clearing, but when I looked again, it was gloomier than ever. I checked before slipping into the bathroom at home. There was no mistake. The rain continued to fall. Once again, I thanked God, the God who now seemed to be answering my prayer.

It was approximately two thirty when the phone rang. It was Al. He was watching the weather as well. But his words of optimism were so different from my thoughts of answered prayer. He was looking west over Ludington, Michigan.

"Lindsey, the sun is popping out from behind the clouds. Look outside. I know you hear the rain, but look out your window. There is a rainbow over Ludington. I think we are going."

"Al, it has rained all day. I am sure the service will be canceled. Please don't be too disappointed. We can walk later today."

"No, you are wrong. I am going to listen for the announcement on the radio station. My mom turned the dial to the right station just before she left. It will give us the answer."

"Okay, Al. Have it your way. But right now, I am going to finish grading papers and prepare for tomorrow's lessons. I have twenty-six first graders who will be eager to learn. Keep me posted."

It was less than an hour until Al called again with the information he had been anticipating. "You are taking me to church. There is no cancellation and you promised"

I had no choice. I was going even if I didn't like it. God didn't answer my prayer. Or did He? I hadn't asked for an all-day rain, and I hadn't asked for the service to be canceled. I had asked for rain, and Al had asked for church. Possibly both of our prayers had been answered in a manner that brought joy to each of us.

My Way

"What does your way look like?" my friends asked. "What in the world are you going to do?"

"I am going to do what I know God doesn't want me to do. You know, the commands He has in the Bible."

"Just exactly what does that look like?" they asked once again. "You still haven't told us."

Immediately, a vivid picture surfaced in my mind, but I was not about to tell them. I didn't have many friends, and the few I had would definitely be condemning and judgmental. I excused myself and walked away. The afternoon was brisk and dreary, and I determined more than ever to do what I purposed in my heart to do. I was looking for love in the wrong places, and the wrong places involved finding a man who would hold me and make love to me. I didn't have to be married; I didn't want a commitment. I wanted love on my terms. I had a definition of love, and I intended to find someone who would fulfill that expectation.

I began to work in a local grocery store deli, and from across the counter, I met the man who just might meet my expectations. It began quite innocently when I took his order and quickly presented him with the needed items.

"Thanks, Lindsey."

"Wait a minute. How do you know my name?" As soon as I opened my mouth, I wanted to take back what I had said in haste. But it was too late. I could only apologize. "I am sorry I was short. I forgot I have a name tag."

"I accept your apology, and in exchange, would you please accept an invitation to go out for dinner?"

"Not now," I responded. "Maybe later."

The smile on his face dimmed. "I have heard that answer too often," he said as he left the deli. I mistakenly thought I would never see him again. Big mistake. He entered the deli weekly after our initial encounter. His order varied, but his question remained the same.

"When are you going to go with me for dinner?"

My response remained the same. "Maybe later."

Although I responded negatively, I began to look forward to seeing him in the deli. He was good looking, muscular, and a gentleman to say the least. He came when the deli was quiet and seemed to enjoy our brief encounters. One evening, he approached the deli and caught me off guard with a different request.

"You don't seem to want to go out for dinner, so I wondered instead if you would like to go hiking in the Ludington State Park? The park is beautiful all the time, but early evenings are gorgeous. The sunset will astound you."

I hiked in the state park often and had never seen my over-the-counter friend. However, I had experienced the brilliance of the orange and yellows that encompassed the sunset over Lake Michigan and knew the enchantment of the wind and the waves.

Without a moment's hesitation, with no doubt in my voice, I responded. "I would love to go."

"Great," I heard him say. "How about Friday evening? Would that work for you?"

I had no excuse especially since I loved the state park so much. I couldn't say no, and when Friday arrived, I found myself pacing the floor, contemplating what to wear. My daughters were attentive and encouraging.

"Just be yourself. After all, he sees you in your deli clothes all the time."

"This is different. There will not be a counter between us. What am I going to wear?"

"We'll help you with your clothes, as if you need our help."

They were right. I didn't need their help. And if I followed their advice I would dress in short shorts and a tank top. That night, I made the choice. I wore dressy jeans, a feminine T-shirt, and my favorite tennis shoes.

I anticipated a late arrival, but my over-the-counter friend Jeff showed up a few minutes early. I was pleasantly surprised, and when I heard him say, "You look great," I was tongue-tied.

The car was quiet, almost too quiet as we entered the park. "Cat got your tongue?"

"No," I responded. Just thinking. It's such a beautiful night."

"Yes, it is. Perhaps we should start walking?"

I agreed, and we were off. "I thought we would walk the skyline trail. It's a lot of steps, but the top of the trail offers a great view of the sunset. What do you think? Are you up for it?"

"Up for it? Yes, I am up for it." That was enough of my ladylike behavior. He thinks I can't make it, and I am about to show him differently. I ran for the steps with Jeff hot on my trail. It didn't take much for him to catch up, but I was able to give him a run for his money.

As we reached the top, Jeff called, "Slow down. This is the best spot to view the sunset."

"Yes, it is. I stop here often when I have enough time to drive out to take my three-mile walk."

"That's another thing you didn't share. You look great behind the deli counter, but I didn't know you walk on a regular basis."

"You never asked, but then, I never told you either."

Laughter filled the air as he grabbed my hand and led me over to one of the trail benches. I felt a tingling sensation flow through my fingers, into my hand, and up my arm. It had been a long time since I had enjoyed the feeling. The sunset that night left us both lingering longer than expected, and when Jeff asked me out for a second date, I quickly accepted.

The night of our second date, I waited by the front window, once again anticipating that Jeff would be late. I giggled as I watched him pull up in the driveway. He was not too early nor too late, but was rather right on time. I quickly stepped away from the window, not wanting to appear too eager. There was no chance of seeing me in the window. My apartment was on the third floor, and 265 steps gave me more than enough time to step away from the window and brush my hair once more. I am not certain who was more eager. Jeff bounded up the stairs. It sounded as if he was taking two steps at a time, and the speediness of his arrival gave me no reason to suspect any different. When I heard the knock on the door, I hesitated for what seemed the appropriate amount of time and then opened the door.

"Hi. Come in while I finish getting ready."

"You look more than ready to me. You are glowing."

"I am not. I am just a little flushed from the heat. Being on the third floor without air-conditioning can be a bit overwhelming."

"Whatever you say. But it looks like you're glowing to me." He left no time for a response. "Are you ready for a hike in the state park?"

"Let me grab my sweatshirt and I will be ready. Which trail are we taking tonight?"

"How about the Lost Lake Trail? Get your things and we can decide in the car."

Once again, we were winding our way out the only dead-end highway in Michigan. M16 curves its way along the Lake Michigan Shoreline out to the state park, and it stops there. The sun was already beginning to drop in the western sky as Jeff commented, "It promises to be a breathtakingly beautiful sunset. I hope we can make it to my favorite spot before the sun sets."

"I think I know the exact spot, and we can make it if we run just a little."

We ran for what seemed like forever. It was getting harder and harder to breathe, and my heart was pounding violently. I had no choice but to slow down. Jeff looked back and immediately slowed down as well.

We arrived at his favorite viewing spot none too early. The sun was already beginning to show its splendor. Tangerines blended with crimsons and sapphires to produce a sunset paralleled to none. We seemed to be alone in the world, absorbed in the splendor of the moment, and when Jeff reached over to kiss me, I responded eagerly.

From his arms to his house took no convincing at all. Before I could respond negatively, I was examining his weights and not soon after lounging on his downstairs sofa. Then, as if in a magical moment, I experienced the *my-way* I had been waiting for, for a very long time. It was a breathtakingly short moment, one etched in my heart and my mind until the time Jeff and I would meet again.

Jeff and I met often after our second date. We walked and talked every time I had an evening off, always finding our way back to his home to lift weights. The excuse was lifting weights, but the ulterior motive was so much more. Where at first I was plagued by guilt, eventually any thought of wrongdoing ceased as my heart hardened to sin.

I began to lift weights almost daily. I found the exhilaration of lifting just a few more pounds a high I couldn't find anywhere else. He was there to encourage me in every way.

"You can lift just a few more pounds if I spot you. Just keep pressing."

"I can do it. Don't help unless I absolutely need it."

"I am not helping unless you are stuck and can't move the bar. I know how to spot."

With the additional support he provided, I began to lift more and more. As the weight on the bar increased, so did the much-needed pounds to my thin frame. Plagued with anorexia from an early age, I now had a reason to eat and gain weight. I had to eat if I wanted muscle mass, and I had to have mass in order to lift more.

I agonized over every pound but continued to eat. Jeff met me at the door one evening after a particularly difficult day battling the addiction that was such a part of my life.

"Lindsey, I have done some research on a body building contest in Northern Michigan. I think you should enter."

"I think you have lost your mind. I am too old to enter any contest."

"Don't say no without investigating this contest for yourself. At least check it out."

Although I had no intention of checking out any contest, I found myself answering, "I will. I promise." As the week progressed, curiosity got the best of me and I started investigating this contest on the internet. What I found intrigued me. The women's divisions certainly were manageable, and I considered myself to have elasticity of skin. I would have to learn to pose correctly, but more importantly, I would have to prepare a musical routine that met the judges' specifications.

On Saturday, my excitement had risen to an all-time high and I almost ran Jeff over as he opened the door for me.

"Hold on. What's all the excitement about? What is going on?"

"I investigated the body building contest you mentioned, and I would like to go for it. I don't know how, but I want to try."

"What did you find out?"

"I can enter into two women's divisions. I can enter by weight, and I can also enter into the masters' division."

"You have done your research. What about the musical routine and posing before the judges? I cannot help you with that."

"I didn't think so, but I called the gym that sponsors this contest, and they have someone who is trained to help me with both. His name is Don, and I'm pretty sure he owns the gym. What do you think about the opportunity?"

"What do I think? I am the one who suggested it, but it's not up to me. You're the one who will have to do all the hard work. It will take hours of discipline and practice. You will have to eat to grow more and then cut weight or body fat just before the contest. Are you committed to that?"

"I am going to do it. I have to give it my best effort."

"All right, let's sit down now and plan a schedule for eating, for lifting, and any goals you may have in order to make this happen."

"I'm ready."

Thus began a rigorous daily routine of weight lifting, cardio workouts, eating, posing, and practicing a musical routine. I could not have accomplished this by myself; but with the help of Jeff and

Don, I grew in bulk, I developed a musical routine, and learned to pose. My children sacrificed. I was gone many evenings, and on weekends, I was traveling back and forth to Traverse City. They often fixed their own meals and watched as I headed out the door for an early morning run or early evening workout. Although they sacrificed, they were excited to see me committed to something that seemed healthy and inspiring.

"We are going with you to the competition. You couldn't keep us away."

"Are you sure you to want to see your mom on stage in a string bikini?"

"Yes, Mom, we are sure. You are going to be terrific."

"How can you be so sure? What if I fail?"

"You won't fail. The only fail is if you don't press through to the finish. That is the only fail at this point. It's just a few more weeks."

As the competition date drew closer, I increased time with my personal trainer in Traverse City and spent less time with Jeff.

There is no other way, I told myself. *I have to travel to Traverse City to practice my musical routine. Hadn't Jeff said this would be a huge commitment?*

As prepared as I was for the approaching competition, I was in no way prepared for the casual feelings I was beginning to have toward Jeff. My eyes were gazing here and there as I entered neighboring gyms. Mingling with other contestants who were being trained at the Traverse City gym offered me a world of opportunities I found exciting and challenging.

To make matters even more complicated, Jeff, who in the past had grabbed me in his arms whenever I entered the door, now casually brushed his lips to my cheek when I approached. It seemed awkward and more than a little confusing. On one hand, I wanted and needed his support, but on the other, I wanted desperately to be independent and to do this on my own.

"I have to be in Traverse City to practice my routine. I can pose with you, but the musical routine is another story. I can't get the rhythm."

"You don't think you have it, but you do. You just need an excuse to ride your motorcycle up to Traverse City and see everyone at the gym."

"If I want to win, I need to take every opportunity to meet with Don, and there is no reason I shouldn't go for the win."

"Just leave it at that. Start lifting."

In my heart, I knew somehow I was losing what had become precious to me, but my way did not include holding anyone precious. I continued to train but distanced myself.

"I have to go to Traverse City. I have to work, and my girls need me home."

"That has never been a priority before. Why now?"

"I wasn't training for a competition before. It takes every waking moment to get in cardio, to pose, and to lift. I have to spend time with the girls."

"If that's more important, I am sorry. I require some time as well. It's a choice you will have to make."

"I've made my decision. I am going to compete, and I am going to spend time with the girls."

I walked out that night realizing that I had just turned my back on my lifting partner and on a very good friend. I told myself I had no other choice. I had to finish what I had started, and competing was far too important.

During the final weeks before competition, I lifted at one of our local gyms. I knew every guy in the gym watched as I lifted. I enjoyed the attention they gave as they spotted for me. I was surprised at how well they gauged my need for that additional lift.

Competition week approached, and my confidence grew as Don assured me of my preparedness.

"You are ready to show. You are ripped, tanned, and your posing is outstanding. It is okay to be nervous, but don't let it consume you. Relax and enjoy this last week. You will be fine."

"I'm not sure I can meet that expectation."

"Do your best. I've never asked you to do more than that."

I tried my best to relax. I followed the plan I had been provided, and on the day before competition, my girls took their paintbrushes and painted me from head to toe with the golden-brown paint I had purchased.

"Mom, this is hilarious. Do you think you should get someone else to do the painting?"

"No, you can do it. Just keep it smooth. No streaks and no globs."

"What if there are streaks?"

"If the paint is not dry, you can smooth it out. If not, I will be splotchy and that is a problem."

"We still think you should get someone else to do this, but it is your call."

"It's too late to be my call. I have already made the call, and I would be much obliged if you would finish the painting. Did I tell you that tomorrow you will have to oil my skin? Won't that be fun?"

"Wait a minute. You didn't tell us that would be part of this job."

"Maybe not, but it is. And it's too late to get anyone else."

"Awful, Mom, simply awful."

Serenity finished the job, with Jonilynn encouraging her with every brush.

"Now I have to walk around and let everything dry as much as possible."

"Yes, no smudges and no streaks."

The day of the competition came too quickly. I slept little, and the music was blaring when the girls walked into the living room.

"Isn't your musical routine fine-tuned enough?"

"Yes, I needed something to fill the time until we leave for Traverse City."

"We'll be ready in thirty minutes."

We arrived at the competition with plenty of time to spare. I was backstage when Jeff walked in with the girls. He was carrying a dozen yellow roses. It was an unexpected surprise, and my legs began to collapse under me. There had been no contact during the past two weeks, and the thought of him showing up hadn't even crossed my mind. He reached out to steady me.

"These are for you. I am so proud of you."

"Thank you for the roses. I'm so glad you came. It means a lot."

"Knock them dead and remember this one thing. It might help you when you are on stage. The audience can look, but they can't touch. If you get too nervous, picture them as naked. That should relax you."

He walked with my girls into the audience, and when I saw them next, I had finished the competition and was receiving the first-place trophy.

Almost Persuaded

I was basking in the light of a first-place trophy when Roy winked at me from across the counter, the same counter that Jeff had reached across over one and a half years prior. I was still ripped from competition, and my tanned body and French-braided hair signified health and youth.

"Where have you been all my life?"

"I have been working in this deli," I replied rather haughtily.

"Wait, I didn't mean to put you on the defense. I haven't seen you here before."

He was right. I hadn't seen him in the store. I only worked on the weekends, but I usually saw the locals in this prominent Ludington Supermarket. Possibly, he wasn't a local or maybe I missed him on my regular shift.

"I'm sorry. Are you a local?"

"I guess so. I live approximately two miles away right off Lake Michigan Drive. Does that make me a local?"

"Yes, I suppose. But I seem to meet all the locals at this deli."

"I don't usually come in on Saturday nights, if this is your night to work. My name is Roy. I am the head bartender at a local restaurant, and I usually work on Saturday nights."

"That explains why I haven't met you. I don't frequent the local bars, or any bar for that matter."

"Does that mean you don't drink?"

"Not necessarily. I just don't go to bars alone."

"Would you consider going out with me for supper and a drink at P.M. Steamers? That is where I work."

My mind raced. I had never met this brown-eyed, muscular, good-looking man, and he was asking me out. The counter in this store seemed so safe, and it had taken Jeff over four months to break down the barriers this counter represented. He must have sensed my hesitation.

"Why don't you meet me at the restaurant if that would make you feel more comfortable?"

"I work every Friday and Saturday night."

"You don't get any nights off?"

"Not unless I ask for them off. It's my regular shift. I teach school during the week."

"And I am a retired Chicago City police officer. I have a badge to prove it. Does that make you more comfortable?"

Was I that transparent? I didn't think so, but he seemed attentive to my facial expressions and my body language. Perhaps they were a display of transparency. He left after giving me his name and contact information.

"I would enjoy having dinner with you next Saturday night. Just give me a call and let me know if you can make it. Hopefully that's enough time if you want an evening off."

"Thanks, Roy. I'll let you know."

I left work and drove to Stearns Park, a favorite spot for teens as well as adults. The beach is terrific, and the sidewalks that surround the park are impeccably maintained and well-lit in the evening. I usually go straight home after work, but tonight I needed to clear my mind. This new man, Roy, kept invading my thoughts, and I wasn't sure I liked it. I stepped out of my jeep, locked the doors, and started to walk.

The evening sky was crowded. A myriad of stars shone on the pavement in front of me, casting an almost magical glow. I felt a slight brush against my jacket and turned my head just far enough to find myself face to face with the man I had just met in the deli. I hesitated as our eyes met. Was he following me? Should I be concerned?

Before I found my voice, Roy broke the silence.

"I never walk on Saturday night. I am always working, but since I didn't work tonight, I thought I would walk. It is such a gorgeous evening. What about you?"

"What about me?"

"Do you usually walk in the park on Saturday evening, or is this a rare occasion?"

Roy hesitated, but only for a moment.

"I'm not following you, if that's what you think. I would enjoy having someone to walk with, but I had no idea it might possibly be you. I've never seen you before tonight. This has to be a coincidence."

I wasn't so certain. I had been stalked before. Could I be so blind again? Or was he right, and this was only a coincidence. I certainly wasn't going to tell him what happened in my past, but I wanted some semblance of safety before walking any farther away from my jeep. Once again, Roy was perceptive.

"Don't forget. I am a retired police officer. I work at P.M. Steamers, have a daughter in Chicago, and a grandbaby on the way. I have been divorced for over twelve years, and I have friends who can vouch for me."

"I don't usually walk on Saturday nights. If my daughters are home, I want to spend time with them. They are very important to me."

"Does that mean you will not go out for dinner with me next weekend? Are your daughters always a priority, or might a guy like me get a chance at being a priority?"

"One dinner does not get you priority rating, but I have asked for next Saturday evening off and there isn't any reason why I won't get it."

"That would be great. Do you want to walk around the park before I call it a night?"

"I guess I could as long as we stay on the path. My girls aren't home tonight."

"Did you think I would lead you off the path?"

I didn't answer. I just started walking and Roy would have to keep up. I never walked for relaxation or for enjoyment. There was always the ulterior motive of exercising and burning carbs. I didn't intend for Roy to stop that. He would just have to keep up with me. And much to my amazement, he was able to keep up with my pace.

Before we said good night, I had promised to contact him with arrangements for the following Saturday evening.

I talked to the girls about this new man I had met. They had been excluded often while dating Jeff, and I didn't want to make the same mistake twice. Perhaps the body building competition played a part in that, but I had experienced some guilt related to my separation from them, and I wanted to be sure they were included. They were eager, and I made plans with Roy for a late-night dinner at P.M. Steamers.

Roy was very different from Jeff. He wanted to wine and dine at expensive locations. He liked the nightlife of Chicago and even Detroit. He wore dress pants, a long-sleeved shirt, and often a tie. My fashion style had changed dramatically after I was raped. I loved my T-shirts and jeans, my sweatshirts and jeans, and my dressy shirts and jeans. Yes, I never left my house without jeans. They were my very identity. Roy did not want to lift weights and made it clear that the gym would not interfere with our time together. He was egotistical and wanted me to be exclusive in dating and exclude my children from our relationship as well. Finally, my jeans and dressy shirts would have to go.

I listened attentively to his demands and decided he was worth the changes I would have to make in my life. All of the changes except one—my daughters still had to come first.

"It's a compromise you will have to make if we are going to keep seeing each other. I will not put my daughters in second place to anyone, including you."

"I can't promise anything. I have always been first when dating."

"I cannot afford to neglect my daughters. My son is older and on his own, but the girls are top priority. I love them and don't want to lose them to anyone."

How could I have been so foolish? A few dinners at the restaurant where he worked, a few walks around his neighborhood, and a few one-night stays were all that I could handle of his stifling, suffocating ways. I wanted to be back in the gym, to be running in the state park, or just hanging with the girls, and he wanted to tie a rope around my neck and chain me to his bed.

My heart pounded as I stood at his front door, waiting for him to open it and greet me. The fear that gripped me was enough to cause me to run, a fear I hadn't felt in a long time. *What was it?* I wondered. And then I remembered. It was the fear I felt on so many occasions during my marriage. It was the fear I felt after the night I was raped. That fear had haunted me for so long. I wanted to run, but I knew in that moment I had to face the fear to tell Roy that I was not going to see him again.

When Roy opened the door, I stood frozen in place. It was if I was reliving past moments all over again. He reached out to welcome me in, and my body came alive. I never waited to be pulled inside.

"It's over. I cannot change the way I dress, I cannot be pulled from my children, and I am not happy staying out of the gym."

"What perfect timing, Lindsey. I was about to tell you the same thing. I am not the person for you. You and I were not meant to be. Let's call it quits before someone gets hurt."

"You are okay with calling it off now?"

"Yes, and it sounds like you are too. Stop by the restaurant once in a while, have a drink, and sit and talk. I'll even buy you that drink."

As I stepped back into the cool afternoon air, my heart was pounding, and my mind was spinning in all different directions. Why did this feel like rejection once again? Wasn't I the one to break this off? Or did he? It would take time to reflect on the answer to that question. And I had more than enough time. Time to spend with the girls, time to lift weights, and time to spend walking with Al. I was no longer chained to this man. And if rejected, then something was wrong because I felt butterflies in my stomach.

Church in the Pink Dance Studio

During the next few months, I reflected often on the subject of rejection. This rejection piece would cause me struggles if I didn't grasp the depth of the problem. But how could I when I didn't understand if there was a problem? Roy had only brought to the surface a topic that seemed to be a holdover from my past. I'm not so sure I would have picked up on it if he hadn't come to the same conclusion about calling our relationship over. It did feel like rejection, and I didn't like it.

I walked with Al often, driven by the desire to stay thin and driven by the desire to compete. I had almost allowed a man to rob me of that joy, and it wasn't going to happen again. Al never gave up on his quest for me to return to God.

"You went to church once. You can again. I will go with you."

"I have no doubt about that. But I have no desire to go to church. You will be the first to know when and if I decide, I promise."

"You keep saying that. When are you going to go?"

"Drop it, Al. I'll decide the answer to that question."

I continued my quest to do things my way, making certain the opportunities of rejection were next to none. That meant I had to keep men at a distance, giving them no opportunity to get close. I walked with Al during the day and walked the waterfront in Ludington at night. It was late in the afternoon during one of those walks that a couple on the beach stepped off onto the waterfront walk. He spoke first.

"I like your helmet. The people we ride with very seldom wear a full-face helmet."

"I never ride without one. I teach the Rider Safety Course, and even if I didn't, I know it's the safe way to go."

"There is no doubt. Statistics prove it. But still, our friends ride with only half helmets."

So far, the short conversation had involved only two. Finally, the woman in the party stepped out.

"My husband is the pastor of a local church. We would love to have you come. You would find that other motorcyclists attend."

"Thank you for inviting me, but no thanks. I am not interested."

"If you change your mind, we meet in the old pink dance studio on the south end of town. Please, won't you consider coming?"

"No thanks."

I finished my walk, convinced that the church nonsense was over. Little did I know that thoughts about church and about God would begin to nag at me. It wasn't Al, because he walked quietly for a while. It may have been God, but I would not have recognized this any more than I would have recognized a song written by James and Garfunkel.

But I was troubled and began to search for this so-called pink church. I wandered through that area until I finally came across the pink building. There was nothing that would make it recognizable as a church, but as I walked around, I came to the conclusion that this must be the church.

Now I had to get up the courage to attend. That would take another three weeks, but one Sunday morning, it happened. I rode my motorcycle into the parking lot, making sure that I was late and would not be noticed. I never went in. I sat on the steps by the door, listened to the music, and caught bits and pieces of the sermon. I left before anyone found me, thinking once again that this casual attendance would satisfy my soul. It did not. I returned the following week and then once more before having the courage to go in.

It was a rainy day, and I still had no intention of going into the church. But this particular Sunday, someone found me sitting on the steps in the rain. As they reached out, I began to cry.

"Why don't you come in? You will find the people loving and kind."

"I cannot come in. No one would want me."

"You're wrong about that one. Everyone would want you, most of all God."

"No thanks. I'm all wet."

"I'm sure the pastor would like to meet you. Please come in?"

"You go in. I will think about it."

I was crying even harder and determined to get back in my car. I pulled a tissue out of my pocket and wiped my tear-stained face. I desperately wanted to leave, but my legs wouldn't carry me. What was wrong?

The stranger at my side took me by the arm and gently steered me to the door. I didn't have any choice. I was entering the church whether I liked it or not.

I have heard that the first time is the hardest, but for me, every time was difficult. I carried the shame and guilt of a broken marriage, the shame and guilt of being raped, and the shame and guilt of living life my way. I eventually started going to a Bible study while still trying to live life my way. I attended those studies but never said a word. Chains kept me bound in a world of shame and guilt no one knew existed.

The entanglement I had developed with the world continued as well. I loved motorcycling as well as teaching the motorcycle safety course for the state of Michigan. I traveled for Ferris State University and taught almost every weekend in May, June, and July.

As if that wasn't enough, during the winter months, I continued to develop my skills in the snowboarding arena. I spent every winter weekend on the slopes, enjoying the view from the mountain peaks, carving the longest runs, and hittin' the terrain parks. I arrived at church on those weekends geared up and ready to hit the slopes, and as soon as church was over, I headed north to the mountain.

Neither of these were wrong, but my life was consumed and that left little time for God and His Word. It left little time for prayer and meditation. In a sense, I was playing both sides of the fence: the world's side and God's side.

At the pink church, I became reacquainted with the truth of God's love and grace. I learned just enough about these attributes to desire to stay away from the my-way journey I had pursued. To accomplish this, I developed a strategy I believed was foolproof. I would isolate when I went to any type of motorcycle training. Yes, I would attend every workshop offered during the training, but as soon as these workshops finished, I would retreat to my room. I would resurface for meals and then back to my room for the remainder of the time.

This strategy worked flawlessly for approximately two years; and then, while attending a training in New York, New York, I was introduced to another rider coach from the Island of Oahu, Hawaii. As our eyes met, every caution sign imaginable surfaced in my mind, but I was defenseless. His charm left me spellbound.

It was a brief introduction, but an introduction that left me watching for Aaron at every workshop I attended. As the first of the three-day training concluded, I realized we had somehow managed to sit at the same table during every workshop and at every meal. We had only talked about motorcycling and training, but I knew the attraction I had for him was mutual and I knew that the opportunity to talk about other things would present itself.

The following morning, I found myself face to face with the man I had come to expect at every workshop. This time, however, he approached me in a more confident manner.

"There is a dinner tonight on the USS *Little Rock*. It is hosted by the Motorcycle Safety Foundation, and I was wondering if you might walk over and have dinner with me. It would be a perfect opportunity to get to know one another."

I hesitated for just a moment before responding. "That would be fun."

"Then let's meet in the lobby of the motel around five, and we can walk over together."

"I will be ready and in the lobby at five."

From the moment I said yes until five in the afternoon when we met for dinner, I anticipated what the evening would be like. I set boundaries in my mind for the portion of the evening after the dinner. I wondered what it would be like if Aaron tried to hold my hand. And if wondering was not enough, I continued to see my date and talk with him at every workshop. My heart was already smitten, and I hadn't been on that first date.

The boundaries that I intentionally set during the day were not easily kept after we spent the entire evening walking, eating, and getting acquainted. It was love at first sight, and I rationalized all boundaries aside in order to attract the man of my dreams.

When he left my room, we were already making plans to spend a few days together in Michigan before he returned to Hawaii. I was following my desires, and although I sensed this was not God's plan, I proceeded.

The conference concluded the following day with dreams of seeing Aaron the following weekend in Michigan. He owned a home in Minneapolis, Minnesota, and after checking on his home, he would take the ferry across to Michigan. It was a perfect plan with only one flaw. He would be staying in my spare bedroom at the apartment. Would I be able to keep my boundaries for four nights?

We were on the phone every day that week; and when Aaron arrived, we greeted each other with a hug and a kiss, a kiss that signified a longing for something much more. As we entered my apartment, he took me in his arms and swept me off my feet. It was all downhill from there. My boundaries evaporated as we hugged and kissed and eventually made love.

The weekend went quickly, and his promises to me were unbelievable. "If you retire, you can move to Hawaii, and after a time, we'll get married."

"I cannot retire for at least another year."

"We can talk on the phone for as long as it takes until you retire. I will wait a year or even more."

"I have to give that some consideration. Can I have some time?"

"No doubt. Take as long as you need. I will wait."

The next morning, Aaron rode his motorcycle onto the SS *Badger* in preparation for returning to Minnesota, and from there, going home to Hawaii. As I watched him sail away, I forgot completely my promise to stay clear of the my-way lifestyle. I cried out from the shore. "I love you. I will see you soon."

It would be 358 days before we would see each other again, but during that time, we talked on the phone daily. That small distraction became a big disruption in choices regarding my relationship with God. I took the focus from God, my rock and my salvation, and placed it on Aaron, a man I barely knew. I never considered the trustworthiness of this stranger. I had fallen in love.

Following My Heart

Never in my wildest dreams could I have imagined that I would be in a jet traveling to Hawaii. I had rehearsed this trip many times during the last few months, planning how I would look, considering the emotions that would arise after such a long absence, and wondering if he would still desire me.

High above the clouds in a United Airlines jet, I wrote in my journal. "I gave up everything to come to Hawaii, I gave up everything to be with you, but I will not give up my soul. I must continue on the path of growing closer to God."

And then I tried to rest. Thoughts of the beautiful islands of Hawaii, a marriage made in heaven, and a new beginning invaded my mind. How could I rest when my entire life was being turned upside down? How could I rest when the fulfillment of a year-long dream was about to take place? As I stepped away from my seat to stretch my legs, I heard the pilot's voice over the loudspeaker. "We will land in Honolulu in approximately one hour. Please begin to gather your belongings in preparation for the seatbelt sign to light. Flight attendants will be coming around to assist."

I quickly returned to my seat, anxiously awaiting the descent into Honolulu. As I looked to the right, I saw the outer islands of Hawaii. I had no idea about their names, but those islands meant we were very close to descending. As the pilot announced the seatbelt sign, my phone came out of my bag. I had promised to text as soon as we landed, and I did not want to delay for a moment.

As the plane touched the ground, the pilot once again called over the loudspeaker, "Enjoy your vacation on Oahu, and if you are traveling to the outer islands, check the board inside the terminal for your departure gate. Thanks for flying United."

I made the landing official by texting Aaron. He would now enter the airport and walk to meet me. My heart was in my throat as I stepped off the airplane and onto the walkway that would lead me to him. I walked down the long walkway watching and waiting. Would he even remember what I looked like? It seemed as if I walked forever, but when our eyes finally met, I knew he hadn't forgotten. We both ran, and as we embraced, any doubts of our love for each other ceased. The touch of his hand, the smell of his skin, and the warmth of his hug had me mesmerized. He gathered my luggage and pointed me in the direction of the car.

"I want to get out of Honolulu before rush-hour traffic. All four lanes of H-1 will be bumper to bumper during that time, and I would rather be at home before it begins."

The sights of Pearl Harbor were visible in the distance as we headed west away from Honolulu. There was so much to see, but that would have to wait until later. A long jet ride, a six-hour time change, and the anticipation of Hawaii left me feeling exhausted. I needed to unpack and rest. I needed to get reacquainted with Aaron.

Those first few days we spent hours together, I rode behind him on his motorcycle to explore various mountain trails. We stopped often to gaze at the beautiful flowers along the road, and he took me to his favorite isolated spots on the island. There, we hugged and kissed and hugged some more. Neither of us could get enough of each other. *Would it always be this way?* I wondered.

After three days on the island, I was ready to visit the Harley-Davidson shop. There was a new Buell waiting for me, and I couldn't wait to ride. Aaron took me to the dealership, and when we left, I was riding a new Buell Lightning XB9SX. How could I be so blessed? I followed Aaron home believing that I would now have the freedom to cruise around the island exploring mountain trails, putting my feet in the ocean, and visiting the obscure spots that only islanders knew existed.

That idea was far from the truth. I could not tell north from south nor east from west on the island. Over and over, I ventured out and then got hopelessly lost. The frustration mounted as I tried to call, but to no avail. If Aaron was not available, I rode around for hours trying to find my way home. What he thought was easy, I found hopelessly difficult.

Three things I had learned about Aaron over the course of the year we spent conversing on the phone.

One: He did movie marathons at least once, more often twice, every week. He paid to get into the theater for the first movie and then avoided the attendants so as not to pay for additional movies. I had no interest in movie marathons, especially when I knew he was not going to pay. His promise to me: "I can be flexible. I will go to one or two movies, and I hope you will go to at least one with me."

That did not happen. Aaron continued to spend five or six hours in the theater on any given afternoon. I tried going to one movie and then leaving, but I would get totally lost trying to find my way back to the house. I was alone and lonely.

Two: Aaron went to church while growing up because his parents sent him. He had not gone for a very long time, but he remembered enough to sound convincing when he talked about God and his faith. His promise to me: "I will go to church with you. I want to be involved in your life. I want you to be happy."

Aaron went with me for approximately six weeks. He then decided church was not for him.

Three: Aaron had a job when I met him in New York, but since that time, he had been fired. He felt he had been wronged and battled everything about his firing in a bitter, resentful manner. I, on the other hand, had been hired by the local community college to teach the motorcycle safety class. I also found a part-time job teaching reading at Kanoelani Elementary School. The irony lay in Aaron's history with the community college and their deep distrust of him. I had to guard what I said about my position with utmost care. Where we once had so much in common, we were now left with little to nothing.

Two things I learned about Aaron during my first three months in Hawaii.

One: He read obsessively. When he was not at a theater, he was on the couch reading. He kept a running count of every page that passed through his fingers. His literature of choice, Vietnam. It was as if he were revisiting his two tours of duty there, as if he were in a state of depression. During those times, he was lost to everyone around him.

Two: He was not a man to be trusted. His former employers did not trust him. His friends did not appear to trust him, and he certainly had not kept the promises he made to me while I still lived in Michigan.

Thus, when Aaron started to take off in the evening, I began to wonder. Where was he going? Who was he seeing? What was he doing? These questions began to crowd out any rational thoughts I may have had. When finally these thoughts consumed me, I locked the doors to the house and waited for his return. Because the front door was locked, he had to enter through the glass slider near the back of the house. I stood there with hands on hips, trying to maintain an aura of calmness.

"Where were you, Aaron?"

"Just out riding."

"You were with someone. I'm certain."

"No, I was alone. I just wanted to ride."

"I can smell something on your clothes, the same scent I have smelled on other evenings. You were with someone."

After more arguing and questioning, Aaron finally answered truthfully. "I was with someone else. Someone I have known for quite some time. I love her."

"You told me you love me. How is it possible to love me and someone else?"

"It's possible. I do love you—"

"I don't want to hear it. Don't say it again. You're lying!"

And then I grabbed my motorcycle gear and headed for the door.

"Where are you going? You shouldn't be riding this late—"

"I will ride if I want to. You can't stop me," I sobbed.

"Can I ride along?"

"I can't stop you from riding, but you'll have to keep up with me."

The tears flowed freely as I snapped the chin strap of my helmet and pulled on my gloves. I left the house with Aaron close behind having no inclination of where I was riding but knowing I wanted to ride as far as possible from the reality of what I had just been told. I could not rid myself of the heavy, oppressive feeling that was beginning to overwhelm me. At times, I felt I would never ride this way again, at times I wondered how it would be possible for me to return to Michigan, and at times I wanted to beg him to love me, to tell me this was a joke. In the three short months I had lived in Hawaii, I had learned to love everything about the island, and I sobbed as the thought of leaving entered my mind.

I rode around the island and into Kaneohe Bay before Aaron motioned me to pull over. It was getting late, and exhaustion caused me to drift on the road.

"You're lost. Please, can I lead you home?

"I don't want to go home. I want to ride."

"I know that, but I don't want you to get hurt. Please, let's go home."

I finally agreed, and we pointed our motorcycles home. Aaron followed the speed limit and watched carefully. When he determined I could find my way, he motioned me to take the lead. Being in front gave him the advantage of watching me for any errors that might indicate I needed to stop. I cried as I rode, agonizing over all the unknowns that were now a part of my future. So many questions and no answers.

For the first time since I arrived in Hawaii, I slept alone while Aaron went downstairs to sleep on the couch. Although my eyes were closed, there would be no sleep. The committee in my head could not be turned off. What would I do? Where would I stay? Why did I believe him in the first place?

Only later would I learn from his roommate that Aaron had been seeing this other woman the entire time he was talking to me on the phone. "Aaron has never been totally honest with you. He was with her until about two weeks before you arrived."

"Why didn't you call me and tell me? You could have gotten my phone number from Aaron."

"I didn't know you. You could have been one of the many bimbos he has had along the way."

"But you know I am not just another bimbo."

"I only learned how special you are after you arrived, but by then it was too late. Aaron isn't the man for you."

"But I love him, and I always will."

The days following my discovery of Aaron's other girlfriend blurred together as I struggled to find some understanding of my circumstances. I tried desperately to make sense of what Aaron had done and was doing. How could he say he loves two women? Why did he convince me to come to Hawaii when he already was seeing someone? But there was no logical reason for any of this. There wasn't a way to justify what had happened to me.

When I wasn't trying to make sense of what had happened, I listened to music on the iPod Aaron had given me for Christmas. I had immediately loaded it with my favorite worship songs, and now the music on the iPod was giving me some sense of peace and serenity in the middle of a very dark time. That Christmas gift gave me the opportunity to tune out the world around me and focus on my only constant—God.

And throughout those first weeks, God reached down and touched me in a special way. He seemed to be reassuring me that I would remain in Hawaii. I had no indication of how, but God seemed to be saying, "There is more for you here, so much more. You'll see."

I didn't see at the time, but I had to trust. I had nowhere to go, no other place to live, and I had two great jobs. I felt desperately alone, but that too would change as God began to fulfill his plan.

Finding Recovery

God's plan included Aaron's roommate, the man who didn't call me, the man who knew Aaron had a girlfriend. He was grieving for me as much as I was grieving for the loss of someone and something I would never have. He watched and waited, quietly looking for an opportunity to invite me to a Friday night meeting of Alcoholics Anonymous. Jacob had been in recovery for many years, and he knew I was not an alcoholic but it was the only thing he thought might help me. The important part was that he wasn't asking me out. Instead, he was asking me to a safe place, a safe place for both of us. AA was where he had to be, and he considered the fact that it might be where I needed to be.

Finally, the night came for him to ask, and when he did, I agreed. I still had not made many friends on the island, and a meeting would give me something to do. Jake and I rode our motorcycles to my first AA meeting. I stood tentatively outside watching Jake's friends greet him. It was evident they had high respect for this man, and they were curious to find out who I was and why Jake had brought me.

After a few introductions, we sat down, and I began to listen. First, I heard that all were welcome. Next, I heard the Serenity Prayer, and finally, someone read the 12 Steps of AA. Words like *powerless* and *surrender* caused me to shudder. I must have some power over what recently happened. Who is this higher power, and how can I surrender to him? I listened carefully as men and women began to share portions of their stories. I heard about the chaos and confusion that alcohol caused in their lives and how they continued on their path of recovery. Many had been in recovery for quite some time. Others had relapsed and were now beginning again, and still, others were attending for the first time.

I heard enough in that first meeting to know that I would be returning. I wanted to hear more about their higher power, and I wanted to hear the 12 Steps once more.

"Jake, can I come back with you next week?"

"Of course! Wait, are you sure? You want to come back?"

"Yes, I want to hear more about the 12 Steps."

"I can give you the Big Book if you want to read the 12 Steps again, and it will answer some of the questions that I'm sure are running through your head. I'm surprised you liked the meeting."

"I'm not sure I liked it, but I heard things that resonated with my married life. Chaos and confusion reigned there as well."

Jake and I went to three or four meetings before he approached me with a second request.

"Alcoholics Anonymous is most likely not where you need to be. I have someone that is willing to pick you up for another type of meeting tonight."

"I like going to AA with you."

"Give this meeting a chance. Al-Anon might be a better suit for you. Please try it?"

I trusted Jake enough to agree to his request. That evening, I attended my first Al-Anon meeting. I told Jake later that I did not like my first meeting nearly as much as I liked the AA meeting. But one thing someone said influenced me to go back. "It's difficult to keep coming back, but healing won't come unless you do. It doesn't have to be this meeting, but try six meetings before you make a decision as to whether you belong.

I tried six meetings. I listened carefully, and tears fell freely at each meeting. I couldn't seem to turn them off. I knew this was where I belonged, but still, I did not say a word. I had so much to learn, but more than that, I did not have alcohol in my background and that seemed to be what Al-Anon was all about.

One Friday evening, shortly after I had attended my sixth meeting, someone shared something that caught my attention. She said, "I had to share my hurts to begin healing. I had to share my story, not my alcoholic husband's story."

My ears perked up as I listened to her story. So much related to mine, except in my situation there had been no alcohol. This Al-Anon group shared in a circle, each person taking a turn as their opportunity arose. There were three people in front of me in the circle. Maybe there wouldn't be enough time? My heart was in my throat as the person in the seat before me finally began to talk. When he finished, everyone turned to me.

"Hi, my name is Lindsey." I fully intended to pass, but words begin to tumble out instead and once started there was no stopping. The Al-Anon group seemed to understand, and they allowed me extra time to share. When the meeting was over, everyone gathered around to hug me. It was a breakthrough that had been long in coming.

Al-Anon meetings did not alter the circumstances of my life, but now there was a shift in focus. I heard stories of men and women who were hurting even more than me. Each week, I heard the 12 Steps, and I began to desire more healing.

The word *sponsor* had been used repeatedly in meetings, and finally, I decided it was time to do something about getting one. I chose a woman who had something I wanted, a peace and calm during the storm. She had serenity. I was elated when she agreed. Her first assignment was to answer the questions related to step one, two, and three from *Paths to Recovery*. We will review them when we meet.

I purchased the book at my next meeting and began to read and answer questions. I desired desperately to stop the downward spiral that I had been on for so long.

Step 1: We admitted we were powerless over alcohol—that our lives had become unmanageable. Someone said, "Think of it as powerless over people, places, and things."

I learned quickly that where I thought I had control, I had none. I was indeed powerless.

Step 2: Came to believe that a power greater than ourselves could restore us to sanity.

Yes, I certainly did need to be restored to sanity. My life had been filled with chaos and insanity for far too long.

Step 3: Made a decision to turn our will and our lives over to the care of God as we understood him.

Wait a minute! Haven't I turned my will and my life over to the care of God? Didn't I do that when I was a young girl? My mind returned to the evening when I made the decision to do life my way. I had been running ever since. Yes, I made decisions that evidenced my desire to turn to God, but I was still trying to do life on my terms. It was time to stop running away and start running to.

I discussed this with my sponsor and she agreed. "If you are feeling a tug in that direction, you may want to follow the lead and realign yourself with your higher power. If you are still running from Him, it quite possibly is time to run to Him."

Adjacent to life changes related to the first three steps came a change in my living arrangements. Aaron continued to stay at the house during the week and travel across the island to his girlfriends on the weekends. Although he did not do anything specific to make the days difficult, his presence alone caused confusion and heartache.

But still, I had chosen to stay in Hawaii, and now, it was time to move forward. When I finally found a shared apartment, I knew I had to grab it. This type of housing was expensive and hard to get. Finding it at a reasonable price had been quite coincidental.

Shortly after I moved, I felt another tug from God. Time to find a different church. Teaching the motorcycle classes kept me busy both Saturday and Sunday, but there had to be a church that had a Saturday evening service. Awareness brought me to searching, and in one of those searches, I saw the sign: "Hope Chapel West Oahu – Saturday-5:30 p.m. service." I looked around but saw nothing that would indicate a church.

The following week, I looked again. Still no indication of a church, but there happened to be a shopping center in that area. I decided to check it out. I rode down in, parked my motorcycle, and started looking. No luck. Finally, I asked someone.

"Yes, indeed, there is a church quite well hidden and next to the gym. Keep walking and you will find it."

It didn't take long to walk over to Hope Chapel. No wonder I hadn't found the church. It was hidden well and looked like a store-front, but it was obviously quite popular. There were many people mingling outside, and it was a weekday. I noted the times and then made plans to attend.

On Saturday evening, I entered the church, and the friendliness of the people blew me away. Never had I been treated so graciously. I loved the worship and thoroughly enjoyed the pastor, but more importantly, I found Celebrate Recovery, a 12 Step program with Christ as the higher power. The Celebrate Recovery meetings were held on Monday evenings, and I couldn't wait to find out more.

When I arrived on Monday night, there were many cars in the parking lot. This wasn't like the Al-Anon meetings I attended. Usually, only eight to ten people attended, and we met in small meeting rooms. When I entered this meeting, it appeared as if there was a church service in progress. I soon learned that every Celebrate Recovery meeting had a time of worship, a teaching lesson, and then small groups.

I listened intently during the lesson and then was invited to join a newcomers' group. There, I learned the ins and outs of Celebrate Recovery (CR). Again, I was asked to come back six times before I decided this was or was not for me. It didn't take six weeks. I already knew CR was for me.

During the next nine months I learned:

- I could live in serenity even if life seemed to be falling apart.
- God loved me unconditionally. He forgave me and called me His daughter.
- I could do nothing to earn His love.
- My mess could be His Message.

My mess was becoming His Message, and I began to consider sharing my story at a CR meeting. My life story continued to remain a secret, and Hawaii might be a safe place to begin sharing, a place far from home. Testimonies (my story) could not be given unless I first wrote it, edited it, and then read it to one person. When these three steps were completed, I would have the opportunity to read it to the large group.

So I began to write. I contemplated carefully what I would share, and I prayed. When stuck, I would talk to my sponsor. Aaron called to check on me often, but even that didn't seem to rob me of the serenity that was now mine. I walked, I lifted weights, and I was growing spiritually. I was living in a peaceful place. Could anything rob me of the peace I had found?

The Diagnosis

I looked down, and there on the toilet paper was one small spot of blood. The following day, I checked for more spotting and not until evening did the next spot appear. Faint as it was, there was blood. I watched closely, and it didn't happen again. However, the uneasiness I felt didn't go away. It had been almost ten years since Dr. Van had said, "You are post-menopausal."

The quiet voice in my head said, "This is silly. It's nothing." I knew I had a scheduled appointment with Dr. Reagan, my ob-gyn, in less than two months. I would be sure to mention it at the appointment. Yet the thought of waiting two months was even more disconcerting than the spots of blood, and on a Tuesday afternoon, I finally called her office.

The receptionist didn't react as if it was silly. She put me on hold, and when she returned to the phone, she said, "Rearrange your schedule. Dr. Reagan wants to see you on Thursday." I marked my calendar and did some rearranging, never considering the urgency that two days represented.

That Thursday, Dr. Reagan performed a biopsy, and when she was finished assured me that everything would be fine.

"There is no way this could be cancer," she said. "You do not fit the stereotype in any area."

She continued by giving me what seemed like 101 reasons why it couldn't be cancer, and I left totally at ease with the situation. I spent the weekend riding with a friend, enjoying a movie, and attending church services. If there was any concern, it didn't show, and it didn't change my behavior. I had a great time.

At school on Monday, I felt my phone vibrate. I pulled it out and looked at the number. I knew immediately it was Dr. Reagan. Although I never answer the phone at school, this call required immediate attention. The receptionist quickly put Dr. Reagan on the phone, and the voice I heard was that of a very concerned doctor. She did not hesitate as she quietly said, "You have a very rare and very, very aggressive form of cancer."

At that point, she did not give me a chance to question. "I am so sorry to tell you this on the phone, but I could not wait to schedule an appointment to tell you face to face." Her call ended promptly, with a promise that she would call back as soon as she finished a scheduled surgery.

When Dr. Reagan called again, she filled in as many missing pieces of the puzzle as possible. There was no way to comprehend what she was saying. I was in shock when she said, "You have an appointment with a gynecological oncologist on Wednesday. It is imperative that we move quickly."

God held me during those first few hours. I brushed back the tears and regained enough composure to finish teaching school. After school, I had to keep a scheduled appointment with the man who was purchasing my motorcycle.

He arrived at the suggested meeting spot just a few minutes late. "Were you concerned that I was not coming? I am so sorry I am late."

"No. I knew you would come. I have other things more important to think about." At that moment, I voiced the diagnosis I had heard from Dr. Reagan only a few hours earlier.

"I just found out I have a very rare and very, very aggressive form of cancer. The prognosis is not good." The tears began to trickle down my cheeks and drip from my chin.

"You could have called. We could have done this another time."

"Yes, I did have to do it. I had to do it today. There is so much to think about, and this relieves me of one thing. I had to come."

"I'll get the money out of the bank. It should only take a moment. Is someone picking you up?"

"No, I forgot to call someone."

"That's fine. I'll bring a friend and we can pick up the motorcycle tomorrow afternoon at your house."

He turned and went into the bank to get the money needed for the transaction. When he returned, he looked at me with a concern that pierced my heart.

"I hope you don't mind, but I called my wife on the mainland while getting the money. She has already called our church, and you are being prayed for as we speak."

I could no longer contain the tears. They began to fall in buckets. I sobbed as I expressed my thanks. He reached out and hugged me, bridging the gap between stranger and friend.

Jeremiah 29:11 kept running through my mind as I struggled to stay composed enough to ride home. "For I know the plans I have for you says the Lord, plans for good and not for evil to give you hope and a future."

I knew this verse to be true, but how could this be a plan for my future and my good? It was too late to call my family on the mainland, and I wasn't certain I could tell them at this point anyway. I needed time to process what I had heard from Dr. Reagan.

As I mulled over God's plan, I remembered the courage and trust that Shadrach, Meshach, and Abednego displayed in Daniel 3:16.

> *O Nebuchadnezzar, we do not need to defend ourselves before*
> > *you in this matter. If we are thrown into the blazing furnace, the God*
> > *we serve is able to save us from it, and he will rescue us from your hand, O King.*
> > *But even if he does not, we want you to know, O King, that we will not serve your*
> > *gods or worship the image of gold you have set up.*

I was being thrown into my blazing furnace, and right then at that moment, I said, "God, I purpose in my heart to follow you no matter what the outcome." Everything seemed overwhelming, but with God, nothing is impossible.

Perhaps the devastation, chaos, and confusion that running from God had caused in my life prompted me to make this choice. Possibly the fact that I had cancer left me with no other choice but to run to God. There was no hesitation.

I left my apartment early in the evening, fully intending to ride until I could ride my motorcycle no more, but God had other plans. He didn't design me to do this alone. He directed my path to where He wanted me to be, a place of healing called Celebrate Recovery. It was there that I began to process the report I had received only four hours earlier. I wept as I shared with the Celebrate Recovery team. "I have a very rare and very, very aggressive form of cancer, and right now, the prognosis is not good."

Prayer is powerful, and as we prayed, I felt God's peace flow through me. I was able to praise Him during worship time, not knowing what my future held but knowing who held my future. I left Celebrate Recovery exhausted and with many questions, but I had peace.

On Wednesday, I met with my oncologist Dr. Carney. Because of the aggressiveness of the cancer, he planned to do a complete hysterectomy. My stomach churned, and it was difficult to focus, but I forced myself to listen as he continued. "Because of the aggressiveness of this type of cancer, chemotherapy will follow."

The little girl in me wanted to scream in terror, and my fingers felt as if I were going to tear holes in the arms of the chair. I wanted to run, but there was nowhere to run. Fortunately, the woman in me spoke up and said, "When?"

I stared into Dr. Carney's eyes as I waited for him to answer. He paused for a long moment and then said. "I have already scheduled the surgery for two weeks from today."

"That's too soon. How am I going to tell my family and friends on the mainland?"

"If I could schedule it sooner, I would. Every day gives the tumor inside you an opportunity to grow. It is imperative that I act quickly."

My eyes began to water, and the breaths began to shorten. I could not, I would not allow myself to panic. I had to regain enough composure to follow the friend who had accompanied me on this visit to her car. I would walk out on my own two feet.

The Journey

The following fourteen days blurred together as I prepared for major surgery. I had to be able to communicate with family and friends. I had to get ready for an unplanned move because my apartment was being sold. I had to, I had to, I had to. It was all so overwhelming.

Dr. Carney's staff recommended Caring Bridge. One of his nurses explained, "This website is specifically designed to connect family and friends during a health event. It is a private, password-protected site, and you can journal as much or as little as you desire on any given day, knowing that this site is safe. You can even add photographs. And your family and friends on the mainland can stay connected by responding to you."

God used Caring Bridge in ways I would never have dreamed possible. In the overwhelming days, the days when I had to face cancer, I journaled. I began by sharing the story of discovering cancer in my body, and then I journaled my deepest thoughts and fears and my trust and hope in God.

Journaling provided an avenue for family and friends to express their concern and their love. They were far away and wanted to understand the challenges I faced. They wanted to know my challenges as well as my victories. The fear, anxiety, joy, and peace all tumbled out on my personal Caring Bridge site. God used His Word to encourage me and others who were reading my pages. I found comfort in Isaiah 43:2–3: "When you pass through the waters, I will be with you; and when you pass through the rivers, they will not sweep over you. When you walk through the fire, you will not be burned; The flames will not set you ablaze. For I am the Lord, your God, the holy one of Israel, your Savior."

As I journaled my way through chemotherapy, I poured out my heart to God. He strengthened me and held me during the roughest of times. Visualize yourself in the palm of someone's hand. That's how it was with God and me. Peace permeated my life.

When my hair began to fall, I remained at peace. Aaron had remained in my life as a friend, and he and I pulled my hair out together. It didn't hurt. It was very therapeutic, and it left no stubbles to deal with. God had a plan. And friends heard.

My bucket list included skydiving, and when I jumped, friends knew. They read about the exhilaration of floating through the air to the ground below. They saw through my eyes the sapphire and indigo hues along the shoreline and the palm trees blowing in the trade winds. Finally, there were pictures of me floating down with my dive master.

When I had a difficult day, my friends knew and they prayed. Their prayers were felt across an ocean. How I loved them for this.

In Michigan, Stephanie was going through chemotherapy as well. I had never met her, but a mutual friend named Hannah was reading my Caring Bridge pages to her as she went to each of her treatments. Hannah called one evening. "Please keep writing. God is giving you strength beyond the impossible, and your words are strengthening the heart of a very dear friend. Just keep writing."

I continued to journal as much for myself as for others. My desire to honor Him was being fulfilled. Obedience brings blessing, and God was blessing me in the middle of a very dark storm.

When I returned to Michigan to visit that summer, I met Stephanie. Her doctor told her she was in remission, and Stephanie couldn't wait to tell me. Hannah had arranged for us to meet at a local restaurant. When I walked into the restaurant, Hannah greeted me with a huge smile and then introduced me to Stephanie. There were tears as we hugged each other. "Thank you from the bottom of my heart for the strength and encouragement your writing has given me."

"It's God," I said. "He gave me the words." God did give me the words, and God used His positioning system to bring Stephanie and me together for such a time as this. The blessing of serving Him in the midst of dark times was beyond my imagination.

While I continued to visit my family on the mainland every summer, I did not visit Stephanie. But Hannah kept me informed of Stephanie's condition. "She is in remission, talks about you, and continues to reread your Caring Bridge pages."

Prior to my third yearly visit, I received a call from Hannah. "Stephanie has cancer again. I don't know how bad, but I wanted you to know." At that moment, God gave me a direct calling for my summer visit. I had to see Stephanie.

Hannah took me to the hospital early on a Thursday afternoon. I had no idea what to expect. Hannah seemed to know so little. When I entered Stephanie's room, I was greeted with a huge hug and many tears. When she was able to gain composure, she said, "I am going home soon. I am tired of the hospital setting, and if I have hospice care, I can go home to get better."

Hannah looked at me and said, "She is going to get better, and she is going to ride her motorcycle again." As I sat on the edge of Stephanie's bed, I listened carefully.

Finally, I asked Hannah, "Would you please get my phone out of your saddlebags? I know I am on vacation, but I should have it just in case someone is trying to reach me."

As Hannah turned and left the room, I immediately took Stephanie's hands and asked her the first of many hard questions. "Stephanie, what is the prognosis? You can be honest with me."

She took a deep breath. "It is terminal." Having voiced that seemed to give her permission to tell me more. We hugged as she continued. "I'm afraid. The doctor has told me to go home and do the things I enjoy doing. He also said it would be wise to have final arrangements in order."

I listened as she voiced her fears and concerns. I hugged her as she continued to cry. Then I offered her the one thing she seemed to need at that moment. "Would you like me to help you with your doctor's request? I have written funeral arrangements for myself."

Again, the tears flowed as she responded. "Would you really do that for me?"

"God has put us together for several reasons, and if you are willing to answer hard questions, I can do this with you." Hannah returned just as I was giving Stephanie a notebook to write down any thoughts that came to mind regarding her final wishes. "I will be visiting my daughter and her family for the next three days, and when I return, we'll spend time together getting this done."

I reached out to Hannah and Stephanie and prayed before we left the room. I marveled at how a website called Caring Bridge could be used by God to bring Stephanie and me together in such a miraculous way.

Stephanie lived her life on earth three more weeks, and I talked to her from Hawaii three times. "The Lord is my Shepherd, I shall not want," were the words she wanted to hear most often. My heart ached for her. How could I bless her? God gave me the answer. "Dedicate Caring Bridge pages to her. Allow the pages to be a tribute to Stephanie and the time you spent together."

The blessings of my story for his glory overflow in such miraculous ways. Stephanie suffers no more, and God used me as an instrument of peace in her last days.

Blessing upon Blessing

The blessings I received as a direct result of my journey through cancer overflow. The summer I met Stephanie for the first time brings back other memories as well. While I was in Michigan that summer, I received a phone call from one of my counselors.

"Can you come to the office? There is someone I want you to meet."

"You want me to come now?"

"Yes. She will only be here for another thirty minutes, so you will have to come right away."

"I'm free, and I'll leave now."

When I arrived, Tim introduced me as God's Magnet. "Everywhere she goes, people are attracted to her but more importantly to the God she serves." And in less than twenty minutes, I shared a portion of my story, the portion that related to circumstances surrounding her life. She then encouraged me to purchase a devotional by Sarah Young entitled *Jesus Calling*. After her recommendation, I wanted that devotional.

I proceeded to check out three local bookstores believing it would be easy to find the book. Not so. My final attempt was a phone call, and finally, I found a bookstore with not just one copy but multiple copies.

They were willing to hold two copies until the following day, and I was leaving for Lansing in less than an hour. The books could wait. I packed my motorcycle gear, checked my tire pressure, and took off for Lansing.

It didn't take long for God to fulfill His plans for the day. Prior to the first exit, I felt a very strong urge to turn around, go to the store, and purchase the book. I followed that nudge and rode back to the bookstore. I was in a quandary as to why today but knew I had to follow the prompting.

When I arrived, the store seemed empty. I found the clerk and asked for the copies that were on hold for me. She knew exactly where they were, and when I was ready to purchase, she asked me an important question.

"Are you in remission or are you still in treatment?"

I wondered how she knew and then realized I had no hair and still looked very peaked. There was no mistaking that I had just finished chemotherapy. I shared just a little of my story with her and then I noticed she was beginning to cry. She spoke once more. "Tomorrow, I start chemotherapy for the fourth time. I'm not certain I can do this again."

"What is your name, and can I pray with you before I leave?"

And so our brief time together ended in prayer, and as I left, customers outside the door began to filter in. It was as if for a moment God provided an opportunity for us to touch each other's lives, an opportunity we would never have again.

As I rode away, I asked, "How did you do that, God? Just how did you make possible the opportunity to meet Dana? I want to know." And then I was reminded.

Obedience brings blessing. Throughout the Bible, people are blessed when they are obedient. Had I not been obedient, I would have missed the opportunity to meet Dana. And what a blessing to have met her!

I am reminded of the young lady I met in the United Airlines Jet as I returned to Hawaii that first summer. She asked the same question that Dana asked, "Are you in remission or are you in treatment?"

I shared a brief synopsis of my journey with cancer, and as I finished, tears flowed. When she regained composure, she stated, "In three weeks, I'm competing in a triathlon in Denver, Colorado. I want to win, but more importantly, I want to compete in honor of you. Will you allow me to do this triathlon in your honor?"

Of course I said yes, and late that summer, I received photographs of this young lady with my name proudly displayed on each of her forearms as she received her trophy for taking first place in the competition. How wonderful to have met her!

One more remembrance that is a reminder of how I am to live my life having had cancer. During the very early weeks as I tried to make some sense of what was happening, of what kind of cancer I had and why the urgency when I was told how grim the prognosis, "Linda, don't go to the internet to find understanding. Stay off because it will scare you too much. Trust your doctors."

And so I did. I stayed off Google. I listened carefully as my doctors explained each step in the process of my treatment. They were thorough in their explanations, and I never felt the need to look elsewhere.

But when chemotherapy was coming to completion, I wondered what next? I am a doer by nature, and while receiving chemo, I was doing something. Finally, I went to Google to search for answers. There, I found that the after in chemotherapy was still doing something. The after was a stage in my journey through cancer, just as real as surgery or chemotherapy. This stage would require just as much trust as the others had.

Shortly after I finished chemo, I attended a day-long workshop at my church. There I heard a speaker comment, "I am a survivor, but I am not certain I am a survivor. Every day I am haunted by what if." That afternoon when I left the workshop, I purposed to focus on God and the miracle of healing He had given me. I would not live in a state of fear, a state of what if.

Following God's Nudge

Once more: what about today?

In July of 2015, I felt God's nudge once again. A specific nudge that called me to a new place, a place I had not lived in a very long time. I felt His calling to return to Michigan, to the exact area where I lived as a child. I hemmed and hawed, not believing this was what He wanted me to do. I prayed and contemplated. How could I leave my beloved Hawaii? How could I leave my Celebrate Recovery family? I had to be certain.

I began looking for a Celebrate Recovery in Michigan, and there were several in the area God seemed to be leading me. I considered all that I was leaving. Everything about Hawaii spoke of recovery; and everything about Michigan spoke of hurts, habits, and hang-ups. But still, God nudged.

Finally, the day came when I heard a knock on my screen door. I saw my landlord smiling through the screen.

"I have something I want to talk to you about," he said.

I invited him in, but he hesitated. "We can talk out here. It's cool in the shade."

It took a minute for him to seemingly muster up the courage, but then the words tumbled out, "I have a family that wants to rent the house. You have always paid your rent on time, but the others in the home are not as responsible. Their rent comes when they have it, not always when it is due."

"You have a family that wants to rent the home? What about me?"

"You will have to find another place to live. I am sorry, but I have to do what is best for me. It will be so much easier if I have one family living here."

"And when do I have to be out of the house?"

"Again, I am sorry, but they want to move in six weeks."

My mind began to spin. I wanted to argue, but I was quickly reminded of what God might be nudging me to do and this seemed a little more than a nudge. Could this be God's way of reaffirming what He had planned in my future? I had two choices: find a place in Hawaii or begin planning for a move to Michigan.

I chose the Michigan option; and within four weeks, I had sold everything, packed what I was shipping including my motorcycle, and was walking down the gateway onto a United Airlines Jet. I didn't know what was in my future, but I did know the God who held my future and He was directing. I had also learned from experience that obedience brings blessing.

Return

More than being blessed, I desired the closeness with my Heavenly Father that accompanies obedience. For so long, I had walked away from Him, and I did not want to make that choice again. So how did God bless me upon my return to Michigan?

It didn't happen immediately, although possibly the blessings did begin to manifest themselves right away. I most likely was focused on buying a car since I hadn't owned one during the eight years I lived in Hawaii, purchasing clothes in preparation for the winter, and finding a job. I also went searching for Al-Anon meetings, a home church, and a Celebrate Recovery Meeting. So quickly, I took my mind off my higher power, Jesus Christ, and placed it on the things of this world.

When I begin to veer off course, God seems to have a way of catching my attention. He did that in June of the following year, just nine months after I moved back to Michigan. His reminder that He loved me was so evident.

I fell asleep driving on one of the busiest interstates in Western Michigan. The speed limit is 70 miles per hour and I had to have been driving that or more. It appears that I hit one guard rail, the car veered, and I crossed all three lanes of the interstate to hit the guard rail on the opposite side. I woke up at some point and took control of the car, bringing it to a stop on the shoulder of the road rather than in the median. God provided an open road with no traffic and a band of angels in the form of air bags to surround me during the entire time. I walked away unscathed. However, my car insurance paid the body shop that fixed my car a little over seventeen thousand dollars in damages. God got my attention that Friday afternoon in June. All I can say is I am amazed.

That same June, I had the opportunity to travel to Haiti on a ten-day mission trip. I believe that God honored a desire I carried with me from my teens, a desire to go on the mission field again. He provided this opportunity through a church mission trip. It was a trip filled with extreme poverty, overcrowded market places, and dangerous roads. It was also a trip filled with beautiful Haitian children, intriguing sights, and opportunities to minister to those in need in Haiti. I went with apprehension and returned with anticipation of the next trip to Haiti.

The second trip took me out of the United State for ninety days, the time allotted for out of country travel without a visa. I had the opportunity to teach and mentor both teachers and students at Grace Christian Academy in Boyer, Haiti. What a joyous three months, not without trials and difficulties, but with blessing upon blessing upon blessing. God has a way of letting me know that I am acceptable, that I am worthy, and that the desires of my heart will be fulfilled. Psalm 37:4 promises, "Take delight in the Lord, and he will give you the desires of your heart."

God gave me the desires of my heart in a much different way when I returned from Haiti.

After sharing a home with others for over ten years, it was time for me to find my own apartment. Two requirements and one wish. The requirements: two bedrooms, one for crafts and one for sleeping, and the other a garage for my motorcycle. My wish—a loft apartment that is not upgraded. Upgrades increase the rental price.

When I voiced my requirements and my wish to the attendant at the apartment complex, she responded negatively. "Loft apartments do not become available often, especially one that is not upgraded. Most often, we upgrade as soon as they become vacant."

My response, "I'll pray about the wish." This was late January of 2017. In early March, I received the call that an apartment was available. "Apartments do not open this quickly often, especially a loft apartment. Yes, there is a loft apartment available. Your God does answer prayers."

The loft apartment is now being used to hold Step studies and Bible studies. It has become a safe haven for women who need a place to stay for a short time. It is my place of serenity, my place to read and write.

Was there a specific reason God brought me back to Michigan? Was it to face the hurts from my past? Was it to give me the opportunity to go on a mission trip to Haiti? These questions cross my mind. On April 12, 2018, my mother passed from life to death. What <u>I Can Only Imagine</u> she now sees face to face. I reflect on the time I spent with her during the past few years. That would not have been possible had I still been living in Hawaii. I rejoice in the half hour I spent with her the night before she passed. That would not have been possible had I still lived in Hawaii.

Finally, I recall the circumstances related to determining a title to this book. Forever ago, I started searching to acquire a title. I prayed, I made title lists, I asked for suggestions, but still did not have a definite answer. No title.

But God has a way of showing up to remind me of how incredibly faithful He is. Just a few weeks prior to putting the finishing touches on the writing, I went to visit a special friend. We talked for a short time and then she hesitantly said, "I was praying for you this morning, and during that time, God told me to tell you something."

I was intrigued. "What did He tell you to tell me?"

"Well, I am not sure why, but He told me to tell you, 'You are worthy.'"

"That's interesting. There are still times when I do not feel worthy, but overall, I believe I do know that I am worthy."

"You have talked about obedience accompanied by blessing, and I just knew I had to be obedient. You are worthy."

In the tiniest fraction of a second, I recalled the reason I had come. My countenance brightened as I said, "God just gave you the title for my book. Your obedience brought me a wonderful blessing. Thank you."

The pages of this book could not contain the blessings God has given in the course of writing it. So often, I am just not aware.

Living beyond this moment—will I ever live in Hawaii again? Will I ever return to Haiti? I do not know. But I do know that my life is not finished. God is directing, and I will follow. "'For I know the plans I have for you,' declares the Lord, 'plans to prosper you and not to harm you, plans to give you hope and a future'" (Jeremiah 29:11).

Is there any reason not to follow?

About the Author

Linda Thompson is a leader in her local Celebrate Recovery Group. Much of her time is devoted to women in Celebrate Recovery or Al-Anon who have experienced hurts similar to hers and are in recovery. Although retired from the public school system, she continues to use her gift to teach in the role of a substitute teacher. She believes children are a gift from God and should be treated as such. If you cannot find her in recovery work or in the classroom, you will find her on her motorcycle enjoying the ride. Linda has three children and eight grandchildren. But most importantly, Linda is a child of God and is dearly loved by her Heavenly Father.

CPSIA information can be obtained
at www.ICGtesting.com
Printed in the USA
FFHW021508161019
55591617-61414FF